CALLED TO HOLINESS

RALPH MARTIN

Called to Holiness

*What It Means to Encounter
the Living God*

IGNATIUS PRESS   SAN FRANCISCO

Contents

Introduction   7

Part One: Meeting God

1. A Holy God   13
2. Mankind: Designed for Holiness   29
3. Our Encounter with God   35
4. The Rejection of Holiness   47

Part Two: Becoming Holy

5. The Gift of God in Christ Jesus   67
6. Conversion   75
7. The Road to Holiness   85
8. The Means of Holiness   99
9. God's Part and Ours   109
10. Holiness and Love   119
11. Holiness and Suffering   125

Introduction

On one occasion Mother Teresa was being interviewed about her life. Reporters sometimes ask people how they feel about their accomplishments, and one reporter asked Mother Teresa about the accomplishment that people most associate with her. "How do you feel about being called a living saint?" he asked. Mother Teresa was not given to self-conscious modesty. She did not say, "Oh, I'm really not as good as people think." Instead she turned the reporter's question around at him. "You have to be holy in the position you are, and I have to be holy in the position God has given me. There's nothing extraordinary about being holy. It is simply a duty for you and for me."

The next question the reporter might have asked but didn't was "What is holiness?" It is a very important question because Mother Teresa was right. We are all called to be holy. But what does that mean?

If we look in the Bible to find out about holiness, we will discover the word *holy* at every turn. The covenant that forms the chosen people is holy, and thus Israel is a holy nation. The places, the camp, and the ground where God is worshipped are holy. His temple is holy, and so are all the things used in his worship—the oil, the vessels, the instruments. When he calls, his call is holy; when he sends messengers, they are holy. When his words are written down, the Scriptures are holy. And of course, over and over, the Bible tells us that God himself is holy.

But what is holiness?

Put simply, when *holy* is applied to created beings, it means "set apart for God". Holy places, clothing, water, ointment, instruments, and offerings are those that are set apart for God. Holy people belong to God. Holy actions and words are vehicles through which God reveals himself.

And when *holy* is applied to God himself, it sums up all the qualities of his greatness. All his vastness and excellence are encompassed by saying, "The Lord is holy." Everything that exists falls into two categories: on the one side there is everything that is, except God; on the other side, God himself. There is everything that has been created, and there is the one who has created everything. There is the universe full of age and immensity, power and life; and there is the holy God, who has given all of it existence.

What does the holiness of God mean for us? What does it mean to meet the holy God? Can we? What happens to us when we do? How can we become holy? These are the questions we will be exploring in this book.

At the outset, it is good to understand that looking into the holiness of God is not an academic exercise or a pastime to satisfy our curiosity. If we turn our attention to God, we will encounter him. If we encounter him, we will be changed.

Some years ago a man who has since become a friend

of mine came to visit the Christian community I belong to. At the time he was not a Christian, although he was interested in knowing God. His first contact with our community was nothing special—just a party that some of us were having. In the course of the evening he asked a few of us questions about ourselves, and we told him about how God had changed our lives. The man did not believe in God, but he realized he was encountering something that went beyond just us. Although he did not understand it, he was encountering the reality and holiness of God.

By the end of the evening, my friend was disturbed. He said to one of us, "I don't know what it is about this community, but I have the feeling that if I stay around here, my whole life will get changed." In the days and weeks that followed, that is exactly what happened. As he continued to encounter the holiness of God, he recognized how wrong the direction of his life was. He turned to God and gave his life back to him. He experienced Christ making radical changes in him. He is with us to this day, serving the Lord and leading a godly life.

Exploring the holiness of God involves more than serious study. God is not a topic to study but a person to meet. And before we begin thinking about him, he has already been thinking about us. When we find ourselves wanting to know more about him, our desire is itself a sign of his work in us. The holy God wants to reveal himself to us and wants to make us holy.

My prayer is that this book may be an instrument that God can use to draw all of us to a life of greater holiness. It is certainly not a comprehensive treatment of the topic of holiness. However, it does treat certain aspects that are not spoken about frequently these days but that are vital for a true understanding of holiness. Please, as you read, don't skip over the Scripture passages I cite. It is amazing what God reveals to us in Scripture of his holiness and his call to us to be holy. His words are far more important than mine.

I would like to acknowledge the contributions of those who helped with this book, especially Kevin Perrotta, whose editorial work helped bring the book to birth much sooner than would have been possible otherwise.

Part One

Meeting God

I

A Holy God

The psalmists of the Bible sing of God's holiness. The angels and saints in heaven worship his holiness. Every Sunday Christians acknowledge his holiness in their prayers and hymns. But what does it mean to say that God is holy?

In one sense, *holy* indicates the "beyondness" and "aboveness" of God. He is great beyond our comprehension. He is lifted up above all that he has made. He exceeds every superlative we can apply to him. *Holy* captures the complete otherness of God. The holy God is different from us, a profound mystery utterly beyond our understanding.

O the depth of the riches and wisdom and
    knowledge of God! How unsearchable are his
    judgments and how inscrutable his ways!
"For who has known the mind of the Lord,
    or who has been his counselor?"
"Or who has given a gift to him
    that he might be repaid?"

> For from him and through him and to him are all
> things. To him be glory for ever. Amen (Rom
> 11:33–36).

But, at the same time, *holy* sums up everything that we *can* know and say about God. It indicates the totality of his excellence, all the qualities of his greatness and goodness that we can gain some understanding of. In this chapter, we will explore some of these qualities.

As we do so, we should keep in mind that knowing God involves more than knowing facts about him. God is a Person, and knowing God means coming to know him as the Person that he is. We can know God personally only because he chooses to reveal himself to us. As his creatures, we could never come to know him if he did not want us to.

Fortunately, God does desire to show himself to us. And one way he does so is as we think about him and sincerely try to understand what he is like. As we ponder the qualities that his holiness encompasses, God will lead us into a personal knowledge of himself. Therefore, to consider the holiness of God is not a mere intellectual exercise. It is a way of turning to the living God and allowing him to show himself to us in the depths of our hearts.

With this in mind, let us reflect on the holiness of God.

The Qualities of God's Holiness

MAJESTY

When we speak of the holiness of God, we immediately reach for the grandest words that human speech can utter.

In the Old Testament, David prayed:

Yours, O LORD, are *grandeur* and *power*,
    majesty, *splendor*, and *glory*.
For all in heaven and on earth is yours;
    yours, O LORD is the *sovereignty*;
    you are *exalted* as head over all.

Riches and *honor* are from you,
    and you have *dominion* over all.
In your hand are *power* and *might*;
    it is yours to give *grandeur* and *strength* to all.
Therefore, our God, we give you thanks
    and we praise the *majesty* of your name (1 Chron
    29:11–13 NAB, italics added).

Majesty is not a word we use often today. The heads of modern bureaucratic governments do not parade around with the majesty of ancient pharaohs and emperors— although, even in our modern world, we have a few examples: the coronation of an English king or queen still evokes some feelings of awe before the symbols of earthly majesty. But for us modern folk the most powerful instances of majesty may be found in the grandeur of creation—the height and beauty of mountains, the glory of the sunrise and sunset, the splendor of the night sky.

The majesty of the universe, far exceeding the scope of human comprehension, gives us an image of the majesty of God. Gazing at the heavens, the prophet Isaiah centuries ago wrote:

Lift up your eyes on high and see:
    who created these?

> He who brings out their host by number,
>   calling them all by name;
> by the greatness of his might,
>   and because he is strong in power
>   not one is missing (Is 40:26).

We moderns should be even more impressed than were people of the ancient world. The universe is much grander than Isaiah, seven centuries before Christ, recognized. Consider the sun, for example. It is 1.3 million times as big as the earth. It is 93 million miles away from us. An airplane traveling at 1,000 miles per hour would take more than ten years to reach it. The heat of the sun's interior, approximately 15 million degrees centigrade, could melt 240 million cubic miles of ice per second.

And as we look beyond our own sun, the scope of God's work is truly staggering. Sirius, the closest star visible from the northern hemisphere, is forty times brighter than the sun, seven times its volume. Polaris, the north star, is a million times the size of our sun. It is four million light years away (one light year is equivalent to over six million million miles). As far as Isaiah could tell, if he had taken the trouble to count, there are four thousand stars visible to the unaided eye. But those are a mere sample of the billions and billions of stars throughout the universe. Our galaxy alone, the Milky Way, is thought to be composed of more than four hundred billion stars, and there may be ten billion galaxies. That, at least, is the extent of creation, the limits of which we have yet to discover with certainty.

And, as Isaiah did say, compared to God the entire universe is like a speck of dust (Is 40:15). Ultimately, even the majesty of the entire universe can hardly be compared to God because he is not merely greater, he is the *source* of all the greatness and splendor of the universe. God has splendor and majesty to such a degree that we might say that God *is* splendor and majesty. All the material majesty of the universe is but a trace of the heavenly majesty of God. Real glory is with him. After God rescued them from the Egyptians, the Israelites sang to him:

> Who is like to you among the gods, O LORD?
> Who is like to you, magnificent in holiness?
> O terrible in renown, worker of wonders (Ex 15:11
>   NAB).

Quite simply, no one is like him. No one is on a par with God. There is an infinite gap between God in his majesty and everything else.

RELIABILITY

As God is great and magnificent, so he is reliable and true. In the New Testament Letter to the Hebrews, we are told not to love money but to be content with what we have:

> For God has said, "I will never desert you, nor will I forsake you." Thus we may say with confidence: "The Lord is my helper, I will not be afraid. What can man do to me?" (Heb 13:5–6 NAB).

This statement sums up the way that God has revealed himself to men and women throughout history, from Abraham and Moses until today: he is faithful.

God's reliability is a favorite theme of the psalmists:

The law of the LORD is perfect,
    reviving the soul;
the testimony of the LORD is sure,
    making wise the simple;
the precepts of the LORD are right,
    rejoicing the heart;
the commandment of the LORD is pure,
    enlightening the eyes;
the fear of the LORD is clean,
    enduring for ever;
the ordinances of the LORD are true,
    and righteous altogether (Ps 19:7–9).

Jesus one day said to a group of people, "Heaven and earth will pass away, but my words will not pass away" (Mt 24:35). God's reliability is infinitely greater than the reliability of anything in his material creation. Granite, which is solid and stable enough for building skyscrapers, is utterly unreliable compared to the reliability of God. Even granite passes away, but God continues forever.

Like all the qualities of God, his reliability is not a fact for us to view distantly and dispassionately. We should take to heart how remarkable it is that the creator of the galaxies promises us, his creatures, that he will never swerve from personal faithfulness to each one of us. To have an influential person act on our behalf—a senator or governor—can make a difference in some situations. To have the creator of the vast universe stand with us can make a difference in *every* situation.

STEADFAST LOVE

The greatest love ever lyricized in a love song, the greatest love ever celebrated in literature, the greatest love ever expressed in any human heroism is pale and weak compared to the enduring love of God. The love of the holy God is immovable, permanent:

> For the mountains may depart
>   and the hills be removed,
> but my steadfast love shall not depart from you,
>   and my covenant of peace shall not be removed,
>   says the Lord, who has compassion on you" (Is
>   54:10).

Moreover, God's love overcomes every obstacle. It is love that is "strong as death", in the words of the Song of Solomon (8:6). Conscious of the fact that Christians do sometimes face death for Christ, Paul told the Christians at Rome:

> For I am sure that neither death, nor life, nor angels,
> nor principalities, nor things present, nor things to come,
> nor powers, nor height, nor depth, nor anything else in
> all creation, will be able to separate us from the love of
> God in Christ Jesus our Lord (Rom 8:38–39).

Thus God's love, unlike human love, is a love on which we can place the weight of our whole lives and never be disappointed. Even the strongest human love is helpless in the face of death. Parents and children, husbands and wives, relatives and friends—all human lovers are helpless in the face of death. No matter how hard we try to hold on to those we love, they die; and their love cannot prevent our death when we reach the appointed moment. But the love of God overturns death. God raises from the dead; God restores life. The love of God shown forth in the death and Resurrection of Christ is the promise that his love is stronger than death for us.

POWER AND WISDOM

The Scriptures often praise God for the power and wisdom he has displayed in his creation. "The heavens are telling the glory of God; and the firmament proclaims his handiwork", the psalmist sings (19:1). "Ever since the creation of the world his invisible nature, namely, his eternal power and deity, has been clearly perceived in the things that have been made", Paul writes (Rom 1:20).

What represents power for us? Nuclear fusion, as in hydrogen bombs and the sun? Fusion is taking place throughout the universe, releasing heat and light in billions of suns. Who put that power there? Who sustains it? God. And God is so much more powerful than the power that he has put in his creation that his power is never used up. God's power is like the fire of the bush that Moses saw, the bush that burned but was not consumed (Ex 3). All the nuclear reactions in a billion galaxies are as nothing compared to the power of God.

> Great is the Lord, and abundant in power;
> his understanding is beyond measure (Ps 147:5).

Human words fail to express the power and wisdom of God because his power and wisdom have no limit.

If we turn from the skies and look at ourselves, we see God's power and wisdom in perhaps an even more marvelous way. Considering the mystery of God's creation of the human person, the psalmist cries out thanks that he is "fearfully" and "wonderfully" made (139:13–18). The human body is an astonishing creation, with its millions of cells, its delicate chemical balances, its complex organs surpassing any man-made substitutes in speed and durability and compactness. With all the human body's shortcomings and vulnerabilities, the very fact that we can move our hands or speak or cooperate with God in the procreation of new human beings is little short of incredible. By making our human bodies the highest evidence of his creative wisdom and power, God has given us an insider's view of his greatness.

JUSTICE

The earth cries out for justice: justice against corrupt judges, against tyrannical rulers, against dishonest businessmen. How often do we say, "That's not right!" about a situation we experience or read about? "It's not right!" is a cry that rings out through history. Yet, where is justice? Human systems of justice are often so late, so inadequate, so unable to right what has been wronged or to discover the wrongdoer or even to care that wrong has been done. Sometimes systems of justice actually perpetrate systematic injustice. Where, in the midst of all this, is there someone willing to judge justly and give people what they deserve? Where is justice?

God alone is entirely just. "Justice and judgment are the

foundation of your throne; kindness and truth go before you" (Ps 89:15 NAB). The justice that the world cries out for is found in God. His Son, Jesus Christ, will come in glory to judge the living and the dead, giving each man and woman what each deserves. Then justice will be done and done perfectly.

God judges on the basis of full knowledge, according to a perfect standard, with complete impartiality, and with the power to reward every good deed and punish every evil deed. No human action in all history will escape the scrutiny of his judgment. No wonder the psalmist sings, "My mouth shall declare your justice, day by day your salvation, though I know not their extent" (Ps 71:15 NAB). We cannot fathom God's judgments; they are more than our human minds can comprehend.

Nevertheless, we can trust in God's justice and look forward to his judgment.

> But the LORD of hosts is exalted in justice [judgment],
>   and the Holy God shows himself
>   holy in righteousness (Is 5:16).

We will see that God is holy when we see how he judges. Our lips will sing his praise, and we will kneel before the holiness of God when we see him judging with justice.

BEAUTY

People will pay millions of dollars for a beautiful painting—and there are tremendously beautiful paintings in the world. People will pay millions of dollars for a home with a sea view or a mountain view, or for a beautiful jewel—

and there are beautiful sea views, mountain views, and jewels. But what is earthly beauty compared to God?

> One thing have I asked of the LORD,
>   that will I seek after;
> that I may dwell in the house of the LORD
>   all the days of my life,
> to behold the beauty of the LORD,
>   and to inquire in his temple (Ps 27:4).

The human heart desires beauty. Beauty is a great delight and consolation. But the beauty of creation and of the works of men and women are dim shadows compared to the beauty of God. If we desire beauty, we should seek God; we should face in God's direction, enter his house, and gaze on his beauty. God is beautiful and the source of beauty.

GLORY

Once, when Jesus was coming into Jerusalem, his disciples and the people living there made a stir. They shouted, "Halleluiah! Hosanna!" The religious leaders who were there said to Jesus, "Tell them to quiet down. They're making a commotion." But Jesus replied that if they did not cry out, the stones would cry out (see Lk 19:28–40). In other words, the glory of God deserves the acclaim of his creatures.

The day is coming when the whole universe *will* cry out the glory of God. The New Testament says that the whole creation is waiting eagerly to see the revelation of the sons of God, because then creation will be freed from its slavery to death and will share in our glorious freedom (Rom 8:19–22). We behold God's glory now, but in a hidden way—as through a dark glass and in the midst of suffering (see 1 Cor 13:12 and 1 Pet 1:6–9).

But one day God's glory is going to be fully revealed to us and in us. We will rise as Jesus rose and be absolutely transfigured. What was mortal will become immortal; what was corruptible will become incorruptible (1 Cor 15:51–55). We will share the glory of God, and the whole creation that is waiting to see it will burst out in songs of praise. "Then shall all the trees of the wood sing for joy" (Ps 96:12). All creatures will cry aloud to God. The Book of Revelation pictures it for us:

> Then I looked, and I heard around the throne and the living creatures and the elders the voice of many angels, numbering myriads of myriads and thousands of thousands, saying with a loud voice, "Worthy is the Lamb who was slain, to receive power and wealth and wisdom and might and honor and glory and blessing!" And I heard every creature in heaven and on earth and under the earth and in the sea, and all therein, saying, "To him who sits upon the throne and to the Lamb be blessing and honor and glory and might for ever and ever!" (Rev 5:11–13).

The prospect of praising God's glory forever may seem overwhelming. God's glory seems too stunning. We may wonder whether we are up to it. Are we spiritual enough to enjoy that? We may hope that there will be some other things to do in heaven besides praising God's glory—reunions with friends and relatives, for example.

But whatever there will be in heaven, it will all be suffused with the glory of God. We will want to praise his glory in our loved ones, his glory in the new heaven and the new earth, his glory in his just judgments. Everyone we meet there will be cause for praise, on account of what God has done in their lives. We will have much to praise God for when we see him face to face and see his just judgment and his beauty. And we will not run out of praise because God does not run out. God never runs out. His glory is forever new.

ETERNITY

My seventeen-year-old son, trying to think about what eternity is, said to me, "Dad, I think something is going to snap in my mind." God's eternity is unfathomable to creatures who are bound by time. Everything we can perceive is in time, but God is eternal. God always was and always will be. He never had a beginning, and he will never have an end.

Have you not known? Have you not heard?
The LORD is the everlasting God,
    the Creator of the ends of the earth.
He does not faint or grow weary,
    his understanding is unsearchable (Is 40:28).

Perennial is his almighty wisdom; he is from all
    eternity one and the same (Sir 42:21 NAB).

God does not change. He was perfect, he is perfect now, and he will always be perfect. And being perfect in the way that God is perfect is not boring. In this life we are always hoping that our ball team will have a perfect season or that our heroes will not turn out to have clay feet or that our favorite music group will not cause a public scandal. But even the best team is far from perfect; and their best, most exciting season is, by definition, followed by a poorer one. Everything in this world loses its excellence, its zest. But God is always at his peak, always fantastic, always the cause of astonishment and delight. God is eternal.

PURITY

In his first letter, John writes:

> That which we have seen and heard we proclaim also to you, so that you may have fellowship with us; and our fellowship is with the Father and with his Son Jesus Christ. And we are writing this that our joy may be complete.
>
> This is the message we have heard from him and proclaim to you, that God is light and in him is no darkness at all (1 Jn 1:3–5).

Later John says:

> And every one who thus hopes [of eternal life] in him [Jesus] purifies himself as he is pure (1 Jn 3:3).

There is nothing twisted, dark, perverse, or selfish about God. He is good, and his love is pure. There is no manipulation or deception or disappointment in his love. We can open ourselves to be loved by God without fear of being violated or taken advantage of. Because God's love is pure, we can yield ourselves to it with full confidence.

> The Rock—how faultless are his deeds,
> how right all his ways!
> A faithful God, without deceit,
> how just and upright he is! (Deut 32:4 NAB).

We could go on to consider God's goodness, knowledge, compassion, providence, patience, and other qualities. But even if we continued for a very long time to think about all that God in his holiness is, we would never come to the end because God never comes to an end. He surpasses all that we can ever say about him. Contemplating the unending greatness and wisdom of God who made him, the psalmist exclaims:

> How weighty are your designs, O God;
> how vast the sum of them!
> Were I to recount them, they would outnumber the
>   sands;
> did I reach the end of them, I should still be with
>   you (Ps 139:17–18 NAB).

It should be our constant amazement that the holy God, infinite in his power and perfection, is indeed with each of us and wants each of us to know him and share in his life and love forever.

2

Mankind: Designed for Holiness

The more we understand about the holiness of God, the more amazed we are likely to become. His majesty, justice, purity, eternity, and goodness surpass everything we can conceive of. The more we understand about God, the greater the difference we notice between him and us. Thus it may come as quite a shock to hear that God wants us to be like him. Here we are, gazing up into the heavens and marveling at his inexhaustible greatness, and he bends down and says to us, "Be like me":

> Consecrate yourselves therefore, and be holy, for I am holy. . . . For I am the LORD, who brought you up out of the land of Egypt, to be your God; you shall therefore be holy, for I am holy (Lev 11:44–45).

But how can we be like God? How can *we* be holy?

The beginning of the answer lies in the way that God made us. As we are told at the beginning of the Bible, God made men and women in his image (Gen 1:27). In our ability to know and reason, to reject evil and choose good, to love, we are made like God. God can call us to be like himself because he has designed us with that outcome in mind.

Of course, we can never be like him in his mightiness, his eternity, his ability to create from nothing. But he created us to be like himself in a measure that is fitting for us. We are supposed to become like God in a human fashion, embodying his goodness, reliability, truthfulness, love, purity, justice, beauty in our human lives. God wants us to become holy in every aspect of our thinking, our speaking, our acting, our working, and our loving.

This commandment and call, first announced in the Old Testament, was given its full expression by Jesus Christ. Jesus summed up his own teaching by saying, "You, therefore, must be perfect, as your heavenly Father is perfect" (Mt 5:48). And the writers of the New Testament echoed his words:

> But as he who called you is holy, be holy yourselves in all your conduct; since it is written, "You shall be holy, for I am holy" (1 Pet 1:15–16).

Scripture does not offer God's call to holiness as a mere option. Becoming holy is the only way we can fulfill the destiny for which God has created us. We have not made ourselves, and we are not free to decide the purpose of our lives. God has made us, and his purpose is the only true purpose we can have. His purpose is for us to be in his presence forever, and he makes it quite plain that holiness is a requirement for this.

Strive for peace with all men, and for the holiness without which no one will see the LORD (Heb 12:14).

Since we have these promises, beloved, let us cleanse ourselves from every defilement of body and spirit, and make holiness perfect in the fear of God (2 Cor 7:1).

This requirement makes complete sense. Heaven would not be heaven unless everyone there were holy. What would heaven be like if people were slandering or lying or had lust in their hearts? Heaven is heaven only because everyone there is in perfect harmony and peace, and harmony and peace come about only when everyone is perfectly in accord with God's will—in other words, when everyone is completely holy.

Notice that *everyone* is required to be holy. Holiness is not just for clergy or for people who come from non-dysfunctional families or for those who have degrees in religious education or for saints in centuries past. As Mother Teresa said to the reporter, "Holiness is a duty for you and for me." Holiness is a fundamental requirement for every human being to enter the kingdom of God. God calls all human beings to holiness because "holiness" is really another way of talking about "salvation". To become holy is to have one's entire personality freed from sin and filled with the love, faithfulness, and purity of God. Therefore, Scripture tells us to "strive" for holiness—to set our sights on holiness, to work for it, to go for it!

The Apostle Paul not only urges us to seek holiness but also speaks specifically about the kinds of behavior that stand in the way:

> Do you not know that the unrighteous will not
> inherit the kingdom of God? Do not be deceived;
> neither the immoral, nor idolaters, nor adulterers,
> nor sexual perverts, nor thieves, nor the greedy, nor
> drunkards, nor revilers, nor robbers will inherit the
> kingdom of God. And such were some of you. But
> you were washed, you were sanctified, you were
> justified in the name of the Lord Jesus Christ and in
> the Spirit of our God (1 Cor 6:9–11).

Paul's list of major wrongs may have more to say to us
than we think at first sight. Paul seems to take slander or
reviling, for example, more seriously than we tend to. He
also means more by it than we may understand. In Scripture "slander" means speaking against someone. That means
not only making false accusations but also telling things
that are true in order to destroy someone's reputation.

When Paul says, "neither the immoral", he uses a word
that Jesus used to indicate sexual immorality in *all* its
forms. By doing so, Paul is alerting us that any kind of
sexual wrongdoing will keep us out of God's presence.
When Paul mentions adultery, he is speaking of sexual
immorality to which is added the breaking of a personal
covenant. The breaking of the covenant relationship of
marriage is thus judged to be a very serious thing. "Sexual
perverts" refers to those who engage in homosexual practices. Homosexual practices are a kind of sexual wrongdoing that involves perversion, a further departure from
God's plan.

"Idolatry" refers not only to worshipping idols but also
to putting anything besides God at the center of our

lives. In modern America we do not have idols in the form of pagan figurines, but we do have many things that beckon us to center our lives on them. Jesus said to seek first the kingdom of God, letting unbelievers worry first about what to eat and what to drink and what to wear (Mt 6:26–34).

First things first. The first thing for everyone, Jesus said, is seeking the kingdom of God, striving for holiness, going after God. Anything else misses God's purpose for us. Jesus says that it is the pure of heart who will see God—that is, it is those who love God above all else, single-heartedly (Mt 5:8). God wants us to put him at the center of our lives rather than making our relationship with him simply one of the many things with which we are occupied.

God in his holiness calls us to holiness. In the beginning he created us to be holy like him. At the end he intends us to be with him in his holy presence forever. And now he is in the process of drawing us deeper into union with him and his holiness.

3

Our Encounter with God

Reader's Digest is one of the more popular magazines in the world, and among *Reader's Digest*'s more popular types of article is the "first-person" story, in which an ordinary person tells about some particularly harrowing experience. The reason first-person stories are so popular is that we all want to know what it is like to meet dangers or challenges that lie outside our own experience. Indeed, this is one of the reasons we read stories of any kind. From the *The Iliad* to *The Red Badge of Courage* and *All Quiet on the Western Front*, from *The Odyssey* to *Typhoon* and *Kon Tiki*, books give us a feel for what it is like to stand on a battlefield or meet the dangers of the open sea.

The Bible gives us accounts of men's and women's encounters with the holiness of God. These accounts help us to understand what it is like to make contact with the God who spread out the heavens and shaped the earth. But unlike stories by Homer and Crane and Conrad, the biblical accounts of people's encounters with God do not merely enable us to have a vicarious experience. The Bible is not a book for armchair seekers after God, the way *Kon Tiki* is a book for armchair adventurers at sea.

God intends the Bible to be a vehicle for our entering into the realities it describes. Of course, the Bible does not literally transport us into the desert of Sinai twelve centuries before Christ. But the Bible's account of Moses meeting God there is designed to bring us into our own encounter with God here and now. We are just as able to encounter God in our armchair (and on our knees) as Moses did on a mountain.

So let us consider some biblical accounts of people's encounters with the holiness of God, and by the action of the Holy Spirit let us take part in their encounters. We begin with the encounter just alluded to—Moses and the burning bush.

Now Moses was keeping the flock of his father-in-law Jethro, the priest of Midian; and he led his flock to the west side of the wilderness, and came to Horeb, the mountain of God. And the angel of the LORD appeared to him in a flame of fire out of the midst of a bush; and he looked, and lo, the bush was burning, yet it was not consumed. And Moses said, "I will turn aside and see this great sight, why the bush is not burnt." When the LORD saw that he turned aside to see, God called to him out of the bush, "Moses! Moses!" And he said, "Here am I." Then he said, "Do not come near; put off your shoes from your feet, for the place on which you are standing is holy ground" (Ex 3:1–5).

We Are Awestruck in God's Presence

Notice that the Lord was concerned to train Moses in how to conduct himself in his presence. It is fitting for us to express by our words and actions that God is overwhelmingly greater and better than we are. God continued:

> "I am the God of your father, the God of Abraham, the God of Isaac, and the God of Jacob." And Moses hid his face, for he was afraid to look at God (Ex 3:6).

Before the awesomeness of God—his unlimited power and majesty and wisdom—fear is a very reasonable response. Who are we to come into God's presence?

Then God said to Moses:

> "Come, I will send you to Pharaoh that you may bring forth my people, the sons of Israel, out of Egypt." But Moses said to God, "Who am I that I should go to Pharaoh, and bring the sons of Israel out of Egypt?" He said, "But I will be with you" (Ex 3:10–12).

In the biblical account of people's encounters with the holiness of God, their awe and expressions of reverence prepare them to hear a word from God, to receive a commission to do something in his service. Very often his directions seem to be more than anyone could carry out. And they would be impossible if God had not chosen the person and was not going to be with him as he obeyed his instructions.

> Then Moses said to God, "If I come to the people of
> Israel and say to them, 'The God of your fathers has
> sent me to you', and they ask me, 'What is his name?'
> what shall I say to them?" God said to Moses, "I AM
> WHO I AM." And he said, "Say this to the people of
> Israel, 'I AM has sent me to you'" (Ex 3:13–14).

This mysterious name that God revealed to Moses was a
way that God identified himself as the source of being.
God is Being itself. The fact that anything at all exists is due
to *God Who Is*. Moses had unexpectedly encountered the
one, living, and true God who made the entire universe.
The encounter, as we know from the rest of the account in
the Bible, changed his entire life. And through Moses God
did fulfill his plan to rescue the Israelites from Egypt.

Next let us consider the description of the prophet
Isaiah's encounter with God.

> In the year that King Uzziah died I saw the LORD
> sitting upon a throne, high and lifted up; and his train
> filled the temple (Is 6:1).

God is pictured as a highly exalted king. His greatness is
shown by the extremely long train of his robe, which
flows in waves behind and before him, filling the entire
throne room where he is seated.

> Above him stood the seraphim; each had six wings:
> with two he covered his face, and with two he
> covered his feet, and with two he flew (Is 6:2).

Even the angels—pure, spiritual beings—covered their
faces before God as they perceived his holiness, just as

Moses took off his sandals and fell down in fear. As the angels hovered near God they sang out:

"Holy, holy, holy is the LORD of hosts; the whole earth is full of his glory" (Is 6:3).

The seraphim saw things as they really are. Unlike us, they were not confused or distracted by passing events, problems, or sins. They saw that everything that God has made reflects his glory as a lake on a summer day reflects the sun. Everything bears witness to God's existence, goodness, power, and love.

And the foundations of the thresholds shook at the voice of him who called, and the house was filled with smoke (Is 6:4).

To encounter the holiness of God is to be shaken to the foundations of our lives, to the very core of our being. Everything about how we think and how we are conducting ourselves is challenged. What does our life look like in the eyes of the holy God?

And I said: "Woe is me! For I am lost; for I am a man of unclean lips, and I dwell in the midst of a people of unclean lips; for my eyes have seen the King, the LORD of hosts!" (Is 6:5).

We See How Unworthy We Are

When we perceive the holiness of God, we also perceive our own sinfulness. We see the difference between God and ourselves, and we feel lost, doomed. We recognize that we are unworthy to remain in his presence. This recognition is true. But God lets us see his holiness even though we are unclean, even though in his presence our sinfulness stands out more painfully than ever before.

> Then flew one of the seraphim to me, having in his hand a burning coal which he had taken with tongs from the altar. And he touched my mouth, and said, "Behold, this has touched your lips; your guilt is taken away, and your sin is forgiven" (Is 6:6–7).

God brings us into his holiness and shows us our sins so he may remove them. God allows us to encounter his purity and see our own impurity, so he may cleanse us and make us holy.

> And I heard the voice of the LORD saying, "Whom shall I send, and who will go for us?" Then I said, "Here am I! Send me." And he said, "Go, and say to this people: . . ." (Is 6:8–9).

God receives us into his presence and cleanses us so that we may then become his servants. This was God's pattern with Moses and Isaiah, and it is his pattern with each of us today.

Now let us consider an encounter with the holiness of God in the New Testament. Jesus has been at the shore of the Lake of Gennesaret, teaching a crowd of people:

> And he saw two boats by the lake; but the fishermen had gone out of them and were washing their nets. Getting into one of the boats, which was Simon's, he asked him to put out a little from the land. And he sat

down and taught the people from the boat. And when he had ceased speaking, he said to Simon, "Put out into the deep and let down your nets for a catch." And Simon answered, "Master, we toiled all night and took nothing! But at your word I will let down the nets" (Lk 5:2–5).

God takes the initiative with us. We may have worked on something without success: trying to turn from this or that sin, trying to care for our family, trying to join with other Christians and serve God together. At a certain moment, however, the Lord will come and say to us, "Do it again, try it again." We must be ready to respond.

And when they had done this, they enclosed a great shoal of fish; and as their nets were breaking, they beckoned to their partners in the other boat to come and help them. And they came and filled both the boats, so that they began to sink. But when Simon Peter saw it, he fell down at Jesus' knees, saying, "Depart from me, for I am a sinful man, O Lord" (Lk 5:6–8).

Jesus purposefully revealed something of his majesty, something of his divinity, to Peter. Peter made the right response. He perceived Jesus' holiness and his own unholiness, and his immediate instinct was healthy: "Leave me, Lord, I am a sinful man."

And Jesus said to Simon, "Do not be afraid; henceforth you will be catching men." And when they had brought their boats to land, they left everything and followed him (Lk 5:10–11).

Only when we understand who God is, only when we encounter his holiness, does the Christian life make sense. Only when we perceive his surpassing beauty and authority does it seem reasonable to leave everything to follow him. God wants us to encounter him, continuing with us the pattern we see with Moses, Isaiah, and Peter, cleansing us from our sinfulness and sending us to do something to advance his kingdom.

Finally, let us read a passage from the last book of the Bible, the Book of Revelation. The author, John, describes various visions:

> [A]bove me there was an open door to heaven, and I heard the trumpetlike voice which had spoken to me before. It said, "Come up here and I will show you what must take place in time to come." At once I was caught up in ecstasy. A throne was standing there in heaven, and on the throne was seated One whose appearance had a gemlike sparkle as of jasper and carnelian (Rev 4:1-3 NAB).

No human words can adequately describe God. Faced with this inadequacy, John offers a picture fantastic and symbolic. God is not literally covered with precious stones. But precious stones image something of the light and radiance of God, which surpass all human words.

> Around the throne was a rainbow as brilliant as emerald. Surrounding this throne were twenty-four other thrones upon which were seated twenty-four elders; they were clothed in white garments and had crowns of gold on their heads. From the throne

came flashes of lightning and peals of thunder; before it burned seven flaming torches, the seven spirits of God. The floor around the throne was like a sea of glass that was crystal-clear. At the very center, around the throne itself, stood four living creatures covered with eyes front and back. The first creature resembled a lion, the second an ox; the third had the face of a man, while the fourth looked like an eagle in flight. Each of the four living creatures had six wings and eyes all over, inside and out (Rev 4:3–8 NAB).

John, we can see, experienced something of the incredible glory of the worship of God in heaven. He is struggling to put this revelation of the majesty of God into human words.

Day and night, without pause, they sang:
"Holy, holy, holy, is the Lord God Almighty,
    He who was, and who is, and who is to come!"
      (Rev 4:8 NAB).

Our Response Should Be Thanks and Praise

In the Catholic liturgy one prayer says that it is "right and fitting always and everywhere to give thanks and praise" to God. John was enabled to see that in heaven all creatures do always give God thanks and praise. Even if we cannot see God's glory as John did, we can be sure that his glory is beyond measure and that at this very moment all the creatures in heaven are worshipping him.

Whenever these creatures give glory and honor and praise to the One seated on the throne, who lives forever and ever, the twenty-four elders fall down before the One seated on the throne, and worship him who lives forever and ever. They throw down their crowns before the throne and sing:
"O Lord our God, you are worthy
    to receive glory and honor and power!
For you have created all things;
by your will they came to be and were made!" (Rev
    4:9–11 NAB).

The elders' crowns are a symbol of earthly authority. Cast down before the throne of God, the crowns symbolize the absolute subordination of all earthly authority to God, from whom all authority comes. The revelation of God's holiness shows his absolute, final authority over everything that he has made. In the end, no intention or plan or effort that opposes him will remain standing. Only men and women who have submitted to his authority and have aligned their wills with his will share his eternal life and glory.

We can note common features in these four encounters with the holiness of God and learn from them. In the presence of a holy God, his creatures prostrate themselves, acknowledging his sovereignty. It is indeed right for us to surrender everything to God, to place ourselves and everything that is ours before him. It is right for us to worship him in silence and in prayer and in song. It is right for us to live praising and worshipping God always.

We also see people become conscious of their unworthiness, their sin. It is important for us to recognize our uncleanness so that God can cleanse us. Many people today claim that they are okay: they do not need anything from God. But the truth is that we need purification. We need God to take the burning coal of the fire of his love and touch us so we can be set free from our sins.

We also see in these biblical encounters that, when people gain a glimpse of the glory of God, he so fills their consciousness that other things are forgotten and they worship him. This is a right response to the holiness of God. We should not merely ask for things from God; we should adore him, prostrating ourselves before him, singing his praises, throwing down our crowns, expressing worship of him.

Finally, encounter with God's holiness is linked with a call to serve him. The people in these biblical accounts, and we ourselves, are sent out to others with a particular mission to bear witness to God and his holiness.

4

The Rejection of Holiness

Moses, Isaiah, Peter, and John were willing to submit to God's will. In the blinding light of God's holiness, they were willing to lay aside their sins and respond to God's commands. But the holy God also breaks in on men and women who remain stubbornly set on their own ways. When he does, they experience the encounter as judgment.

The Bible offers many illustrations. Very early in its history of mankind the Bible speaks of wickedness reaching such a point on the earth that God "repented" of having created man (Gen 6:6). God's human "experiment" had failed. God was not being glorified; rather, the human race was blighting and perverting his creation. Eventually, God decided to destroy the race. Men would have an encounter with him that would publicly demonstrate his holiness and their wickedness, and they would perish in the encounter. Indeed, the flood came, and only a few were spared from destruction.

But God's judgment had a saving purpose. When God's holiness encountered mankind's sinfulness in the flood, he revealed his mercy as well as his anger. Because of Noah's righteousness, God decided to give mankind another chance. With his wooden boat, Noah brought a nucleus of the human race safely through the flood waters of God's judgment. In doing so, Noah pointed toward the perfect mercy that God would reveal in Christ. Noah himself prefigured Christ—the righteous man who, by the wood of the Cross, would lead men and women out of God's judgment of sin and through the waters of baptism into a new life with God.

In the destruction of the cities of Sodom and Gomorrah, we see again the same judgment of sin and revelation of mercy (Gen 18:16—19:28). Again God decided to execute his judgment on people who insisted on rejecting his ways. God allowed Abraham to know of his plans, and Abraham was very concerned because his relatives were living in Sodom. Abraham asked God to spare the city if there were even a few righteous men in it. Abraham was a good bargainer, and God agreed to save the city if only ten righteous men could be found in it. But God could not find that many, so he led Abraham's relative, Lot, and his family out of the city. Then he destroyed it.

As in the case of Noah, this encounter with God's holiness meant punishment for those who resisted God's will but salvation for those who obeyed him. Again the encounter pointed to God's revelation of mercy in his Son. Both Lot and Abraham prefigured Christ—Lot as the righteous man living among the unrighteous and Abraham as the righteous man interceding for the salvation of others.

We Disregard God's Holiness at Our Own Peril

Later in the Bible we are told of the punishment that a single man experienced in an encounter with the holiness of God. The incident occurred while the the ark of the covenant was being brought into Jerusalem. The ark—a box containing the stones on which God had written the Ten Commandments—had been captured by the enemies of Israel. When it was returned, King David wanted to bring it into Jerusalem and give it a place of honor. However, he disregarded God's instructions that, as an expression of reverence, the ark should be handled only by priests and Levites. Instead, David had the ark loaded on an oxcart manned by ordinary laymen, including one named Uzzah. Here is what happened:

> And when they came to the threshing floor of Chidon, Uzzah put out his hand to hold the ark, for the oxen stumbled. And the anger of the LORD was kindled against Uzzah; and he smote him because he put forth his hand to the ark; and he died there before God. And David was angry because the LORD had broken forth upon Uzzah (1 Chron 13:9–11).

God did not want David to have an overly familiar or casual approach to him. By ignoring God's instructions for giving the ark special handling, David was not showing proper respect for God. And without proper respect for

God, there was no proper relationship with him. On reflection, David recognized this. He called some priests together and said to them:

> "Because you did not carry it the first time, the LORD our God broke forth upon us, because we did not care for it in the way that is ordained." So the priests and the Levites sanctified themselves to bring up the ark of the LORD, the God of Israel. And the Levites carried the ark of God upon their shoulders with the poles, as Moses had commanded according to the word of the LORD (1 Chron 15:13–15).

We may surmise that God's final judgment of Uzzah was merciful, since Uzzah's intention was apparently to serve God and he may have been acting on inadequate knowledge of what God wanted. But the lesson is clear: it is foolish for a creature to encounter the holy God without an attitude of obedience and reverence. Without proper submission to God, the encounter with his holiness brings punishment rather than blessing.

We could examine many other Old Testament examples of the punishment experienced when unrepentant men and women encountered the holiness of God. Indeed, the whole story of the people of Israel is an ongoing encounter with the holiness of God, often demonstrating the judgment that comes from rejecting his ways. God revealed his holiness to Israel in gracious and saving ways, but by and large his people turned away from him.

God demonstrated his holiness by letting their enemies triumph over them, taking them away into captivity and destroying their city and temple. But rather than dwelling on these Old Testament examples, let us look at the New Testament. First, let us consider a letter from Paul to the early Church at Corinth:

> The Lord Jesus on the night when he was betrayed took bread, and when he had given thanks, he broke it, and said, "This is my body which is for you. Do this in remembrance of me." In the same way also the cup, after supper, saying, "This cup is the new covenant in my blood. Do this, as often as you drink it, in remembrance of me." For as often as you eat this bread and drink the cup, you proclaim the Lord's death until he comes. Whoever, therefore, eats the bread or drinks the cup of the Lord in an unworthy manner will be guilty of profaning the body and blood of the Lord. Let a man examine himself, and so eat of the bread and drink of the cup. For anyone who eats and drinks without discerning the body eats and drinks judgment upon himself. That is why many of you are weak and ill, and some have died. But if we judged ourselves truly, we should not be judged. But when we are judged by the Lord, we are chastened so that we may not be condemned along with the world (1 Cor 11:23–32).

Paul is talking to Christians about partaking of the Eucharist. In the Eucharist we eat the Body and drink the Blood of the Lord. We encounter the holy God in a profoundly personal and intimate way. Paul warns us that if we enter this encounter unworthily, without repentance and seriousness, we risk judgment rather than blessing. God will punish us for our own good—"he chastens us to keep us from being condemned"—but his judgment will be no less real for all its merciful purpose.

An account in the Acts of the Apostles shows how serious the consequences may be when a person disregards the holiness of God:

> But a man named Ananias with his wife Sapphira sold a piece of property, and with his wife's knowledge he kept back some of the proceeds, and brought only a part and laid it at the apostles' feet. But Peter said, "Ananias, why has Satan filled your heart to lie to the Holy Spirit and keep back part of the proceeds of the land? While it remained unsold, did it not remain your own? And after it was sold, was it not at your disposal? How is it that you have contrived this deed in your heart? You have not lied to men but to God!" When Ananias heard these words, he fell down and died (Acts 5:1–5).

The narrative goes on to say that Sapphira in turn also lied to Peter. And she too fell dead at his rebuke.

Ananias and Sapphira did not have to give what they had to the Church. Their sin lay not in keeping their money but in lying about what they had done. Lying to the Church meant lying to God, who filled the Church with his presence by the Holy Spirit. Disregarding the holiness of God, they came under his judgment.

These passages from 1 Corinthians and the Acts of the Apostles may strike us as out of keeping with the message of God's mercy in the New Testament. But Paul's warning to those who receive the Eucharist unworthily and the story of God's judgment on Ananias and Sapphira for their dishonest behavior in his presence are very much in line with the rest of the New Testament.

Some people think that the "Old Testament God of justice" has given way to a "New Testament God of mercy": people were punished in the Old Testament, but now God accepts everybody; we can do whatever we want if we are "basically good" persons. Just about everyone will get to heaven. But, in fact, there is only one God. The same God made the Old Covenant and the new one.

God reveals himself more deeply and clearly in the New Testament, but he himself does not change. Under either Covenant, to turn away from the living God is to choose death; to resist his holiness with stubbornness is to encounter judgment. In the New Covenant God draws closer to us and shows his mercy more richly. But if we scorn his mercy, we will experience his judgment. Indeed, the New Testament makes clearer than the Old Testament what the consequences of obedience and disobedience will be—life and reward not only in this life but forever, or death and punishment not only in this life but for all eternity.

The New Testament takes up and repeats the Old Testament's teaching about God's judgment, applying it to those who encounter God's mercy in Christ. For example:

> I want you to know, brethren, that our fathers were all under the cloud, and all passed through the sea, and all were baptized into Moses in the cloud and in the sea, and all ate the same supernatural food and all drank the same supernatural drink. For they drank from the supernatural Rock which followed them,

and the Rock was Christ. Nevertheless with most of them God was not pleased; for they were overthrown in the wilderness. Now these things are warnings for us, not to desire evil as they did (1 Cor 10:1–6).

The Scriptures Are Clear about God's Judgment

The punishment of God's people in the Old Testament is preserved in Scripture as an example to keep us from the wicked desires that bring down the judgment of the holy God. If we do not avail ourselves of these lessons, we are refusing one of God's greatest mercies to us. Out of his concern for us, God is showing us his attitude toward sin. He is giving us a merciful warning about how unrepented sin will be dealt with.

> [A]s it is written, "The people sat down to eat and drink and rose up to dance." We must not indulge in immorality as some of them did, and twenty-three thousand fell in a single day (1 Cor 10:7–8).

There are consequences to sin, and these consequences are clearly spelled out throughout the Old and New Testaments. Jesus said to those who saw his works but refused to believe in him, "You would not be guilty of sin if I had not come and spoken to you. But as it is, I have come and spoken to you, and now there is no excuse" (see Jn 9:41).

We will not be able to say on the day of judgment, "Nobody ever told me what was right and what was wrong and what the consequences would be." From the beginning to the end of Scripture and through two thousand years of Christian tradition, the message is clear; indeed, the basic principles of right and wrong are written in our hearts (see Romans 2:14–15). God gave his Son for the forgiveness of sin, but if we do not avail ourselves of that forgiveness and live in the holiness that he now makes possible, what will remain for us except punishment?

> We must not put the Lord to the test, as some of them did and were destroyed by serpents; nor grumble, as some of them did and were destroyed by the Destroyer. *Now these things happened to them as a warning, but they were written down for our instruction,* upon whom the end of the ages has come. Therefore let any one who thinks that he stands take heed lest he fall (1 Cor 10:9–12).

It is possible to reject the grace of Christ. It is possible to reject God and live for our own desires, as the Jews did in the desert, and experience the consequences. Their offenses against the holiness of God are not strange or archaic. We too are tempted to turn away from God by making our stomach our god, indulging in sexual immorality, testing the Lord rather than trusting him, complaining about his will for us rather than thanking him for his love and care.

Almost daily the media report to us the latest developments in the unfolding of the AIDS epidemic. While there are certainly innocent victims of the epidemic, the vast majority of those affected have engaged in sexual immorality—whether heterosexual or homosexual—or have abused drugs. Once again, in our own day, we see vividly illustrated the same lesson of the Jews in the desert after the Exodus when 23,000 died in one day because of sexual immorality: the wages of sin is death.

We Need to Guard Our Hearts

Grumbling may not seem too serious an offense when we compare it to sexual immorality. But complaining is a symptom of bitterness taking root in the heart. The author of the Letter to the Hebrews admonishes us to see to it that "no root of bitterness spring up and cause trouble, and by it the many become defiled" (Heb 12:15). Turning away from God often begins with grumbling and complaining—blaming God, disregarding his holiness, and losing a proper fear and reverence of him.

If we harbor this bitterness, we abandon a position of adoration and submission, and arrogance and pride creep in. Subtly we become our own god. Instead, we should imitate Job, who suffered greatly but refused to curse God. He said, "The LORD gave, and the LORD has taken away. Blessed be the name of the LORD" (Job 1:21). Even while he searched for an explanation, Job submitted patiently to the trials God allowed him to endure.

The permanent relevance of Old Testament judgments is cited not only by the Apostle Paul:

Did God spare even the angels who sinned? He did not! He held them captive in Tartarus—consigned them to pits of darkness, to be guarded until judgment. Nor did he spare the ancient world—even though he preserved Noah as a preacher of holiness, with seven others, when he brought down the flood on that godless earth. He blanketed the cities of Sodom and Gomorrah in ashes and condemned them to destruction, thereby showing what would happen in the future to the godless (2 Pet 2:4–6 NAB).

Every example of the destruction of the godless in the Old and New Testaments is thus an image of the final destruction of the godless at the great judgment that will usher in the end of time. Then we will all have a decisive encounter with the holiness of God. If we have repented of evil and embraced Christ, the Lamb who takes away the sins of the world, we will come before God transformed and holy. And we will enter his presence forever. If we have persisted in sin, we will be consigned with the fallen angels to the pits of darkness in hell. Either we will live with the holy God, or we will suffer apart from him. There is no third alternative.

This is what will happen in the future. This is human life seen from God's point of view. We need to form our minds according to his view, which is communicated in his word. We need to see ourselves and the world with God's understanding, so that we can live with this eternal perspective.

This perspective is not popular today. Most men and women have their attention focused on this life apart from eternity. If people think at all today about God's judgment, they tend to be complacent. Many people have lost sight of the holiness of God and have created their own image of God, formed according to human desires. From scholarly theologians, religious educators, and ordinary people, one hears a rejection of the New Testament's portrayal of the holiness and judgment of God. A God who hates wickedness, whose very presence is judgment for those who stubbornly reject him? "That's not my God", many reply. "My God would never send anyone to hell. My God would never punish anybody. My God accepts people as they are. My God affirms people."

As the editor of a Catholic diocesan newspaper put it: "I believe there is a hell, but that nobody is there . . . ten out of ten will go to heaven. It is inconsistent that a loving God would allow people to damn themselves" (*U.S. Catholic*, May 1983, p. 8).

This kind of response is rebellion against God—the substitution of a lie about God for the truth. Often this remaking of God is rooted in an unwillingness to obey him. Rather than accepting God's invitation to be made clean, some people rebel, preferring to stay in their sin, rationalizing it and finding teachers who rationalize it. The New Testament says, "People with itching ears will seek teachers to tell them what they want to hear" (2 Tim 4:3).

If I point out what Scripture actually says about God's holiness and judgment, some people become angry and accuse me of being a "fundamentalist", not because of my way of interpreting Scripture but simply because I really believe what it says. In fact, what Scripture says is often easily understandable. This is not to say that we do not need the Church and Christian tradition to guide us in understanding the Bible or that there are not many questions that biblical scholarship can helpfully illuminate.

Scripture Tells Us What Is Necessary for Salvation

But the basic messages of Scripture are not complicated. The gospel is understandable by the simple as well as the learned. Luke tells us that Jesus rejoiced in the Holy Spirit because the wise and the clever did not see the coming of the kingdom, but God was revealing it to the merest of children because they were willing to receive it (Lk 10:21). If God wants to save the human race, doesn't it make sense that what is necessary for salvation can be understood by the ordinary person?

Indeed, Scripture speaks plainly about God's holiness and mankind's sin. Sophisticated attempts to blur the Bible's simple message of God's mercy and judgment in Christ are not based on superior interpretation but on a desire to rationalize a lack of faith and repentance. God's view of such attempts can be surmised from Jesus' rebuke to theologians of his day who, he said, used cleverness to release people from the central obligations of the law, such as honoring one's parents. Thus these religious leaders refused to enter the kingdom themselves and blocked the way for others (Mk 7:8–13; Mt 23:13–14).

In the Gospel writers' descriptions of Jesus' coming, the people's rejection of him, and his response, we see more clearly than anywhere else the encounter of the holiness of God with unrepentant men and women. While some people responded to Jesus, most people did not. As he said, they preferred to remain in the darkness of their sinful behavior rather than to come into his light (Jn 3:19). The holiness of God came to men and women, but most closed their hearts to him.

Jesus foresaw the outcome. By rejecting the only one who brings true peace and life, they would end in disaster. He had come to save them from judgment; having refused him, what else could save them from the consequences of their departure from God? Jesus did not take vindictive delight in the prospect of their destruction. He had come in compassion to save them, and he departed from them in sorrow. But he will return at the appointed time in glory as the great and holy king to judge the living and the dead.

Shortly before his death, Jesus wept over the city of Jerusalem. He knew that if the people persisted in rejecting him, they were going to experience God's judgment in a concrete and painful way (Lk 19:41–44). He prophesied that the city of Jerusalem would be destroyed. And we know that in 70 A.D. Roman armies arrived, encircled the city, and captured it.

Hundreds of men were crucified. Women and children were burned to death on the roof of the temple. The temple itself was destroyed. The walls of the city were torn down. To this day one can go to Rome and see the Arch of Titus, with its sculptures showing the triumphal parade after the sack of Jerusalem and the Roman soldiers carrying the lamps of the temple. These things actually happened. Jesus' prophecy was fulfilled. God's judgment was carried out in this present New Testament age, which stretches from the First to the Second Coming of Christ. God demonstrated his justice in this age of his relationship with mankind, the age in which we are now living.

God Will Not Be Mocked

From beginning to end, the Scriptures show us that God is not mocked. God is not a fool, not weak or inconsistent. God is holy. His holiness is demonstrated throughout history as men and women encounter him, either repentantly for their salvation or unrepentantly for their destruction. We will encounter his holiness inescapably at the end of time.

Paul tells us:

> Do not be deceived; God is not mocked, for whatever a man sows, that he will also reap. For he who sows to his own flesh will from the flesh reap corruption; but he who sows to the Spirit will from the Spirit reap eternal life (Gal 6:7–8).

In his infinite patience and mercy, God gives us chance after chance. But in the end, he will not be disregarded. Those who obey him will live forever. Those who scorn him and die in their sins will be separated from him forever. God and his law are real. Life is not a game. Christianity is not a game. Something is at stake; indeed, everything is at stake. That is why the Word became flesh. Christ's coming was not just a gesture. It was an almost incredible act of self-giving, so that we might escape judgment and achieve the fulfillment for which we are created. So much is at stake that Christ was willing to endure the Cross. If we accept the forgiveness he offers us, we find life forever. If we reject it, what remains for us is judgment.

The New Testament makes it clear that because the

grace given in the New Covenant is even greater than that given in the Old Covenant, to profane the holy things of God and to treat them lightly under the New Covenant is deserving of a worse punishment than approaching God unrepentantly under the Old Covenant. The New Covenant is made in the Blood of Jesus Christ, which is more precious than the blood of bulls. Its law is higher than the law given by Moses. *Thus violations of the New Covenant will receive a greater punishment than violations of the Old Covenant.* This point is made especially strongly in the Letter to the Hebrews:

> For if we sin deliberately after receiving the knowledge of the truth, there no longer remains a sacrifice for sins, but a fearful prospect of judgment, and a fury of fire which will consume the adversaries. A man who has violated the law of Moses dies without mercy at the testimony of two or three witnesses. How much worse punishment do you think will be deserved by the man who has spurned the Son of God, and profaned the blood of the covenant by which he was sanctified, and outraged the Spirit of grace? For we know him who said, "Vengeance is mine, I will repay." And again, "The Lord will judge his people." It is a fearful thing to fall into the hands of the living God (Heb 10:26–31).

The New Covenant in Christ is God's final offer. He wants to have mercy on us; mercy is his deepest desire. But if we refuse his offer of mercy, then he will not endlessly rescue us from the consequences of our choice. If we hear the truth about Christ and respond to it but later turn our backs on him, we have rejected the only way that our sins can be forgiven. It is not that God ceases to love us or stops offering us forgiveness. But he will not force us to accept his offer of love and forgiveness. Later, the writer of Hebrews says:

> Strive for peace with all men, and for the holiness without which no one will see the Lord. . . . For you have not come to what may be touched, a blazing fire, and darkness, and gloom, and a tempest, and the sound of a trumpet, and a voice whose words made the hearers entreat that no further messages be spoken to them. For they could not endure the order that was given (Heb 12:14, 18–20).

The writer is referring to the Israelites' encounter with the holiness of God at Sinai. God had spoken to Moses and the people and given them the Ten Commandments.

> Indeed, so terrifying was the sight that Moses said, "I tremble with fear." But you have come to Mount Zion and to the city of the living God, the heavenly Jerusalem, and to innumerable angels in festal gathering, and to the assembly of the first-born who are enrolled in heaven, and to a judge who is God of all, and to the spirits of just men made perfect, and to Jesus, the mediator of a new covenant, and to the sprinkled blood that speaks more graciously than the blood of Abel (Heb 12:21–24).

In Christ, God reveals his presence to us in a way that is outwardly less fearsome but even more profound than at Sinai. The Israelites had an external experience of the presence of God, manifested in thunder and lightning. In Christ, God brings us right into his presence, where he is surrounded by his angels and saints, where Jesus and the Blood he shed on the Cross stand forever opening the way to the Father. But the Scripture warns us that while the New Covenant is not accompanied by the same terrifying signs, it is even more holy. Any violation of it is incomparably serious:

> See that you do not refuse him who is speaking. For if they [the Israelites] did not escape when they refused him who warned them on earth, much less shall we escape if we reject him who warns from heaven. His voice then shook the earth; but now he has promised, "Yet once more I will shake not only the earth but also the heaven." . . . Therefore let us be grateful for receiving a kingdom that cannot be shaken, and thus let us offer to God acceptable worship, with reverence and awe; for our God is a consuming fire (Heb 12:25, 28–29).

Thus the Old Testament and, even more, the New Testament show us a holy God, whose presence is a humbling and purifying fire for those who are willing to repent of their wrongdoing and adore him. But it is a fire of just judgment for those who reject his offer of mercy and cling to their own ways.

Part Two

Becoming Holy

5

The Gift of God in Christ Jesus

We have been considering God's holiness and the fact that God has created us to be holy. We have noted some lessons from God's encounters with people described in the Bible. We have seen that people who spurn God's offer of forgiveness and obstinately refuse to lead a holy life will eventually experience his judgment.

What response can we make to all this?

If we have caught even a faint glimmer of God's holiness, we are likely to be pained at the thought of our own sins—our pettiness, selfishness, and malice, the ways we have closed our hearts to others and have knowingly hurt them to secure our own advantage, pleasure, and fulfillment. But not all sorrow for sin is useful. After writing a sharply critical letter to correct some abuses in the Church at Corinth, Paul wrote to the Corinthians:

> For even if I made you sorry with my letter, I do not regret it (though I did regret it), for I see that that

letter grieved you, though only for a while. As it is, I rejoice, not because you were grieved, but because you were grieved into repenting; for you felt a godly grief, so that you suffered no loss through us. For godly grief produces a repentance that leads to salvation and brings no regret, but worldly grief produces death. For see what earnestness this godly grief has produced in you, what eagerness to clear yourselves, what indignation, what alarm, what longing, what zeal! (2 Cor 7:8–11).

There is a kind of grief over our sins that is mainly self-concerned and self-pitying. It becomes stuck in bitterness and regret. Rather than opening us up to God, this kind of grief turns us in on ourselves in despair—and even defiance. "Well, then," we may say to ourselves, "I *am* a selfish person. Deep down, I *am* looking out for Number One. I am *not* a loving person—and there's nothing to be done about it!"

It is amazing how our "flesh"—our fallen human nature—can take what is intended in God's plan to be a conviction of sin, a grief that leads to repentance, and perversely use it as an excuse to keep us from repentance. It is both sad and frustrating to see in ourselves and our fellow men the foolishness and disguised pride that put our judgments above God's Word and say, "We can't repent. We can't change." Instead, we should humbly cast ourselves on God's mercy and ask for his forgiveness and mercy once again.

But there is a godly kind of grief, which brings a proper fear of the Lord. We feel sorrow for our wrongdoing because we see how we have spit in God's face and despised his laws, how unjustifiably we have hurt other people and have failed to use opportunities for doing good, how great a mess we have made of the life God has generously given us. The more profound our perception of God's holiness, the more profound the perception of our own sin. And the more we are genuinely grieved by our sins, the more receptive we become to hearing God's word of forgiveness.

Grief over our sins, however, brings us face to face with a very big question. How can we be any different from the way we are? Encountering God's holiness and acknowledging our sins provide a tremendous *motivation* to change. But how? How can *we* be holy?

Our failures to obey God point to the fact that even our best efforts do not take us very far toward holiness. The older we get the more clearly we see that we simply do not have the resources for holiness within ourselves. Being like God from the heart is beyond our natural reach. Holiness seems like a majestic mountain range looming before us as we travel over a plain. The nearer we come, the more imposing the mountains become until they tower above us. The possibility of climbing them becomes more remote the more accurately we are able to gauge their height.

We Must Look to the Cross of Christ

In our predicament, there is only one place to look, and that is to the Cross of Jesus Christ. In Jesus' Cross we see the definitive encounter between the holiness of God and the sinfulness of the human race: we see the perfect goodness of God and the wickedness of man's rebellion against him. In the Cross we find God's creation of the one way out of our sinfulness, the one point of entry into a life of holiness.

On Jesus were laid all the hate and folly and blindness and greed and fear and self-concern that the world contains. All human wrongdoing was focused on him—the pure, holy, unspotted Lamb of God. And he bore it away.

The deadly consequences of human sin were made public once and for all. God's perfect love and forgiveness were made equally obvious. And his love and forgiveness triumphed.

At the Cross Jesus was completely obedient to the Father. Because Jesus was God as well as man, his obedience had cosmic repercussions. It reversed the effects that followed the disobedience of the first man:

> Then as one man's trespass led to condemnation for all men, so one man's act of righteousness leads to acquittal and life for all men. For as by one man's disobedience many were made sinners, so by one man's obedience many will be made righteous (Rom 5:18–19).

Apart from Christ we are alienated from God and locked in sin even when we try to obey him by our own power. We are simply lost apart from Christ. But Christ opens a new life with God for us. United to Christ and filled with the Holy Spirit, we can begin to live in obedience, holiness, and love.

A life of obedience, by definition, involves our efforts at obeying. But our being able to enter this life of obedience and our being able to live it out come to us not through our efforts but as pure grace. Life in Christ is a gift:

> For the wages of sin is death, but the free gift of God is eternal life in Christ Jesus our Lord (Rom 6:23).

Because of sin, we deserve to die. But the gift of God to us in our sin is eternal life in Jesus Christ.

God calls us to respond with faith and obedience to his action in the death and Resurrection of Jesus. The Apostle Paul said that God had sent him to bring the nations to "obedience of faith" in Christ (Rom 1:5). Through faith and obedience we become united to Jesus and share in his death so that we might share in his Resurrection:

> Do you not know that all of us who have been baptized into Christ Jesus were baptized into his death? We were buried therefore with him by baptism into death, so that as Christ was raised from the dead by the glory of the Father, we too might walk in newness of life. For if we have been united with him in a death like his, we shall certainly be united with him in a resurrection like his. We know that our old self was crucified with him so that the sinful body might be destroyed, and we might no longer be enslaved to sin (Rom 6:3–6).

When we repent and believe and are joined to Jesus, he reaches deep inside us and makes a radical change in us.

I have known many men and women over the years who were locked in bondage to sin in all its varieties—

lying, stealing, sexual immorality, substance abuse, unrighteous anger, hatred, bitterness, hostility, and sorcery. Through faith in Christ, repentance, and participation in the life of Christ, they have all at once or gradually been set free, so they can live righteous lives that are pleasing to God and a blessing to their fellow men.

The sinful aspect of our nature is crucified, crushed, and broken when we repent and turn to God. We are made able to live a holy life—a life that will culminate in our fully sharing in Christ's Resurrection:

> But you are not in the flesh, you are in the spirit, if in fact the Spirit of God dwells in you. Any one who does not have the Spirit of Christ does not belong to him. But if Christ is in you, although your bodies are dead because of sin, your spirits are alive because of righteousness. If the Spirit of him who raised Jesus from the dead dwells in you, he who raised Christ Jesus from the dead will give life to your mortal bodies also through his Spirit which dwells in you (Rom 8:9–11).

In Christ a new life has been opened to us, a life of union with God, a life of sonship, holiness, and love, a life in the Holy Spirit. This life exceeds our expectations. We tend to think in terms of getting to be a little bit better. But God has revolutionized our lives by uniting us to his Son in his death and Resurrection. He has given us his Spirit and the prospect of an eternally glorious future.

God has transformed our situation so completely that Scripture even now calls us "holy ones"—saints! (2 Cor 1:1; Eph 1:1; Phil 1:1). This does not mean that we are perfect yet, but that we belong to God through what Jesus Christ has done for us and through our taking hold of him. God has already taken possession of us by his Spirit. In Christ we have already passed from death to life. And so, right now as Christians, we *are* God's holy people, *right now* we are the temple of his presence on earth by the Holy Spirit dwelling within us if we have believed and have been baptized and have obeyed him.

No creature can be holy without God. Isaiah could not have been holy if God had not sent the angel to put the burning hot coal to his lips. Peter could not have continued in the presence of Jesus unless Jesus cleansed him and made him able to follow him (see Jn 15:3). We could not live in harmony with God if he had not acted to conform us to the death and Resurrection of Jesus and had not poured his Holy Spirit into our hearts. Because he has done just that, we can respond to him with faith and obedience, thanks and praise. We can respond by living a life more and more characterized by holiness.

6

Conversion

God has done so much for us in his Son's Incarnation, death, and Resurrection. Let us examine what our response must be.

First of all, responding to Christ appropriately involves a *total transfer of authority*. We move from living under one authority to living under another. It is a little like changing citizenship (see Col 1:15).

If we have not been aware of the authorities under which we have already been living, the concept of a transfer to another authority may be puzzling. "We're free individuals, aren't we?" we may ask. The answer is yes, but not entirely. Apart from Christ, our freedom is undermined at every turn by competing influences, usually not to the degree that we lose our freedom altogether and are no longer responsible for our actions, but seriously enough that our experience of freedom is deceptive.

What other authorities have some control over us? For one thing, the people around us have a great deal of influence on how we think and what we do. We model ourselves on other people and pick up ideas, values, and desires from the society we live in—a society that often does not recognize God. Then, too, our own deep-rooted tendencies to look out for ourselves—to get ourselves noticed and appreciated, to control others, to satisfy our sexual urges, to nurse resentments, and so on—lead us away from holiness in ways that we may or may not understand or even notice. And finally, evil spirits deceive and tempt us. We might never know this unless God reveals it to us. But Scripture clearly teaches that, having rebelled against God, human beings have fallen under the dominion of evil spirits who are at war with him.

In other words, the world, the flesh, and the devil thwart our efforts to do what is right. Without Christ, we inevitably come under the influence of these external and internal forces. We find that we are not completely free to obey God, even when we set out to do so; rather, we are under authorities in rebellion against him.

To become a Christian is to be transferred from the sway of these forces to the lordship of Christ. The world, the flesh, and the devil continue to exist and trouble us, but they no longer have the claim on us that they did before. We have died to them and have been brought into life as subjects in God's kingdom.

We ourselves must ratify this transfer. Like a person renouncing his former citizenship and becoming the citizen of another nation, we must repudiate the authorities in conflict with God under which we have been living. We must declare our intention to live under the authority of the new government we are embracing, the lordship of Christ.

We Must Completely Reorder Our Loyalties

Second, transferring our allegiance from one authority to another means a *complete reordering of loyalties*. Our loyalty to God and Christ becomes paramount. Family, career, friends, organizations, causes—all become subordinate to our loyalty to Christ. This loyalty to Christ was already clearly foreshadowed under the Old Covenant by God's call to the Israelites to be absolutely loyal to him. A passage from Deuteronomy speaks of this loyalty in terms of "observing" his commands, "loving him with all your heart and soul", "following and fearing" him, holding fast to him alone:

> Every command that I enjoin on you, you shall be careful to observe, neither adding to it nor subtracting from it. If there arises among you a prophet or a dreamer who promises you a sign or wonder, urging you to follow other gods, whom you have not known, and to serve them: even though the sign or wonder he has foretold you comes to pass, pay no attention to the words of that prophet or that dreamer; for the LORD your God is testing you to learn whether you really love him with all your heart and with all your soul. The LORD your God shall you follow, and him shall you fear; his commandment shall you observe, and his voice shall you heed, serving him and holding fast to him alone (Deut 13:1–5 NAB).

There is no suggestion here that uncompromising loyalty to God is a special ideal for the few. God addresses his command to all his people. The only right way to relate to the holy God is to be completely loyal to him.

Disloyalty to God is not taken lightly:

> But that prophet or that dreamer shall be put to death, because, in order to lead you astray from the way which the LORD, your God, has directed you to take, he has preached apostasy from the LORD, your God, who brought you out of the land of Egypt and ransomed you from that place of slavery. Thus shall you purge the evil from your midst (Deut 13:6 NAB).

Loyalty to God necessarily means purging evil from our own lives. In my own life and the life of my family, I've found it very helpful—in fact, necessary—to eliminate a lot of popular music, television, magazines, and secular movies, which do not help to accomplish our goal of following Christ with undivided loyalty. Being exposed to a lot of current popular entertainment inevitably weakens our desire to follow Christ, dulls our thirst for prayer, and lulls us into accepting immorality as normal and "not so bad". It also addicts us to electronic stimulation, making us dissatisfied with the daily faithfulness and self-denial of living the Christian life.

Whatever we have allowed into our life that weakens our loyalty to Christ and leads us away from him must be dealt with. The Israelites were called to deal severely with disloyalty:

> If your own full brother, or your son or daughter, or your beloved wife, or your intimate friend, entices

you secretly to serve other gods, whom you and your fathers have not known, gods of any other nations, near at hand or far away, from one end of the earth to the other: do not yield to him or listen to him, nor look with pity upon him, to spare or shield him, but kill him. Your hand shall be the first raised to slay him; the rest of the people shall join in with you. You shall stone him to death, because he sought to lead you astray from the LORD, your God, who brought you out of the land of Egypt, that place of slavery. And all Israel, hearing of it, shall fear and never again do such evil as this in your midst (Deut 13:7–12 NAB).

No human relationship, no matter how important, should take precedence over our relationship with Christ. No matter how genuine our love for someone is, it is never right to allow anyone to draw us away from obedience to Christ. Unhappily, many people are weakened in following Christ because of the displeasure or scorn or disinterest of people they are close to. They are not bold enough to say, with Joshua, "As for me and my house, we will serve the LORD" (Josh 24:15).

Much of the confusion we have in the Church today stems from people wanting to follow Christ but fearing to displease their friends or neighbors or coworkers or theological peers or seminary buddies or fellow clergy. Even in some Church circles today, making clear one's loyalty to Christ can get one ostracized and branded a "fundamentalist". Many people let themselves be enticed into disloyalty to Christ out of this fear of offending other people.

Peer pressure is something that not only our children

have to deal with. We fall into it, too. How easy it is to remain silent when a dominant person in a group of which we are a part negatively characterizes Christian teaching on marriage and family life. We too many times allow Christ and his teaching to be mocked. How easy it is to "join the crowd" in watching a particular movie or singing a particular song, even if it glorifies immorality, blasphemy, and rebellion.

Our Supreme Loyalty Is to Christ

Nobody has a rightful claim on us to cause us not to follow Christ. It is never right to fail to follow Christ because son or daughter or beloved wife or husband or intimate friend asks or pressures us to do so. Our supreme loyalty is to Christ and his teaching. Jesus himself is very clear on this point:

> If any one comes to me and does not hate his own father and mother and wife and children and brothers and sisters, yes, and even his own life, he cannot be my disciple (Lk 14:26).

Loyalty to Christ means not only that we must guard against letting others draw us away from Christ but also that we must conduct ourselves toward other people in a way that pleases Christ. We need to be husbands, wives, parents, and children who live as servants of Christ. We are not to be servants of people's emotions or to be manipulated by desires; rather, we are to be servants of Christ, who serve as spouse or child or employee as Christ wants us to. Our spouse, children, parents, colleagues, and friends are gifts from God. We should desire to give glory to him as we relate to them in a way that pleases him.

Third, placing ourselves under Christ's authority and making him the supreme object of our loyalty means a *radical restructuring of our priorities.* We need to put first things first, second things second, and so on.

A lot of the confusion and frustration people experience today is due to their having many of the right elements in their lives, but having them in the wrong order. Jesus has some telling things to say on this subject. For example, he told this parable:

> There was a rich man who had a good harvest. "What shall I do?" he asked himself, "I have no place to store my harvest. I know!" he said, "I will pull down my grain bins and build larger ones. All my grain and my goods will go there. Then I will say to myself: You have blessings in reserve for years to come. Relax! Eat heartily, drink well. Enjoy yourself." But God said to him, "You fool! This very night your life shall be required of you. To whom will all this piled-up wealth of yours go?" That is the way it works with the man who grows rich for himself instead of growing rich in the sight of God. . . .
>
> That is why I warn you: Do not be concerned for your life, what you are to eat, or for your body, what you are to wear. Life is more important than food and the body more than clothing. Consider the ravens: they do not sow, they do not reap, they have neither cellar nor barn—yet God feeds them. How much

more important you are than the birds! Which of
you by worrying can add a moment to his life-span?
If the smallest things are beyond your power, why be
anxious about the rest? Or take the lilies: they do not
spin, they do not weave; but I tell you, Solomon in all
his splendor was not arrayed like any one of them. If
God clothes in such splendor the grass of the field,
which grows today and is thrown on the fire tomor-
row, how much more will he provide for you, O
weak in faith! It is not for you to be in search of what
you are to eat or drink. Stop worrying. . . .

Seek out instead his kingship over you, and the rest
will follow in turn (Lk 12:16–21, 22–29, 31 NAB).

That is pretty clear, isn't it? Stop worrying. Let God
care for you. Now that you have recognized his authority
over you and have declared your loyalty to him, trust his
love for you. The unbelievers of this world, who do not
recognize his authority and do not make loyalty to him
uppermost, are always running after the things of this
world. Your Father knows that you need these things.
Instead, be primarily concerned with his rule over you, his
will for you. "Seek first his kingdom", and the rest will
follow in turn.

We Need to Put God First

After we are converted to Christ, we continue to have
many of the same concerns. We continue to need food,
clothing, and shelter. We still have to work. Numerous
interests and responsibilities may play a part in our lives.

But the way we prioritize all these things changes. We seek first the kingdom of God, making God and the coming of his kingdom our first priority. Then the other things that we need take their rightful place. God will provide them in the ways he wants to. Our heart is to be focused primarily on the kingdom of God.

A friend of mine recently told me how he had just turned down a pay increase and greater responsibility in his company so he could continue to have an early morning prayer time with his wife and children. He knew it was a lifeline for them in keeping their lives centered in God. The new job would have required him to leave the house too early to continue the prayer time. I've known many people—including myself—who have made similar choices in order to "seek first the kingdom" and have been blessed with the "other things" as well.

Jesus is very encouraging to those who put God first:

Fear not, little flock, for it is your Father's good pleasure to give you the kingdom. Sell your possessions, and give alms; provide yourselves with purses that do not grow old, with a treasure in the heavens that does not fail, where no thief approaches and no moth destroys. For where your treasure is, there will your heart be also (Lk 12:32–34).

Conversion means accumulating real treasure—holiness, the reward of God, the hope of being with God forever, the joy of seeing his kingdom come into the lives of men and women. When we are converted to Christ, we come to share his concerns and find that our true fulfillment lies in serving God. Our priorities become growing in holiness, serving others, doing the will of God, using the opportunities—our span of life, our relationships, our resources—that God has given us to further the coming of his kingdom. He may have entrusted us with a lot or a little. Whatever he has given us, he expects us to use it under his direction, to give him glory and to build up his kingdom. As we respond in this kind of way, we will grow in holiness.

7

The Road to Holiness

The road to holiness begins with conversion to Christ. It leads through our whole life in this world, and it reaches its end only when we pass from this world into God's presence forever.

Our initial conversion does not produce instantaneous perfection. When we are brought into God's kingdom at our initial conversion, we bring a lot of the world, the flesh, and the influence of the devil in with us. And so we must begin a process of change, allowing Christ to become Lord in every part of our life. Thus initial conversion opens the door to a life of ongoing conversion. Whether we begin as infants or later in life, we enter this life of conversion through faith and baptism. We receive a new birth, forgiveness for our sins, and are cleansed in the Blood of Christ. We receive the gift of the Spirit. We are initially made holy by God's saving grace. Then we continue to live this new life with faith and obedience as God's life grows in us. We grow in holiness, which is a lifelong process.

The process involves more than a series of adjustments. It involves transformation. Becoming holy means more than altering some details of our behavior; it means thorough personal renewal. God not only wants to see a change in our external actions; he also wants to bring about in us an inner purity of heart that reflects his own goodness.

In my own life, I can see how Christ first worked in me so I would not act out my negative reactions in certain relationships. Then he began to give me greater freedom not to "react" internally but to look to him for wisdom and love so I could be a servant in those relationships. I am far from perfect, but it is encouraging to see what Christ is about in me and in all of us who seek to serve him in our relationships. He changes our mind and heart, our way of looking at things, when we turn to him.

This was one of Jesus' main concerns in the Sermon on the Mount:

> You have heard that it was said to the men of old, "You shall not kill; and whoever kills shall be liable to judgment." But I say to you that every one who is angry with his brother shall be liable to judgment; whoever insults his brother shall be liable to the council and whoever says, "you fool!" shall be liable to the hell of fire. . . . You have heard that it was said, "You shall not commit adultery." But I say to you that every one who looks at a woman lustfully has already committed adultery with her in his heart (Mt 5:21–22, 27–28).

Jesus is concerned not only with our avoiding murder, adultery, and other kinds of wrong behavior. He wants us to become the kind of men and women who do not yield themselves to such sinful desires. This means learning to nip sin in the bud where it begins—in the mind. It means training ourselves to turn away from unrighteous thoughts. As we do this, the Lord changes our mind and heart.

God Wants to Transform Our Mind and Heart

Jesus made this point about inner transformation forcefully:

> You have heard that it was said, "You shall love your neighbor and hate your enemy." But I say to you, Love your enemies and pray for those who persecute you, so that you may be sons of your Father who is in heaven; for he makes his sun rise on the evil and on the good, and sends rain on the just and on the unjust. For if you love those who love you, what reward have you? Do not even the tax collectors do the same? And if you salute only your brethren, what more are you doing than others? Do not even the Gentiles do the same? (Mt 5:43–47).

We all have our share of enemies and persecutors, and to love them is very difficult. Not to react in kind when they injure us but to respond with the love of Christ—that requires a change inside us as well as a change in our outward behavior.

Crucial to this process is a transformation in our thinking. Scripture speaks of "taking every thought captive to Christ" (2 Cor 10:4–5). When we first turn to Christ, we certainly do not come with all our thoughts "captive", or shaped, by him. We have to begin looking at things as he looks at them. Learning from his word in the Scripture, we have to take on his mind. Paul writes:

> I appeal to you therefore, brethren, by the mercy of God, to present your bodies as a living sacrifice, holy and acceptable to God, which is your spiritual worship. Do not be conformed to this world but be transformed by the renewal of your mind, that you may prove what is the will of God, what is good and acceptable and perfect (Rom 12:1–2).

Living as we are in a world alienated from God, having tendencies in ourselves to turn from him, and having evil spirits trying to deceive us, we are in great need of spiritual discernment. We must learn how to distinguish what is from God and what is not, evaluating things with the wisdom of Christ. This requires more than mere information; it requires a renewal in our whole way of looking at life.

For example, many of the decisions we are faced with in daily life can be rightly decided only if we keep in mind the overall goal and purpose of our life: to live and die united to Christ; to help as many others as possible to do so also. Decisions about whether to go to a particular activity or not, to attend a certain school, to take a certain job, or to move to a certain city need to be considered in light of how they would affect our goal of living and sharing life in Christ.

If going to a certain event would be more a temptation for us than an opportunity to witness to our faith, we should not go. If taking a certain job would make it difficult for us to have a daily prayer time, spend time with our family, and participate in a Christian support group, we should not take it. Keeping in mind the long-term goal—the eternal perspective—is very helpful for discerning and deciding rightly in the daily circumstances of life.

God Wants to Set Us Free

Because growth in holiness means inner transformation, it brings moral freedom. When we set out on the road of holiness, we immediately run into opposition from our own tendencies toward wrongdoing, which vary depending on our past, our family history, our circumstances. Our sins are forgiven, but our inclinations to sin—while weakened and no longer having dominion over us—are not abolished. The Lord wants to free us from these obstacles; and, as we grow in holiness, we find ourselves increasingly free to follow him.

Many people do not grasp this connection between holiness and freedom. Holiness seems like a burden to them, a set of narrow rules limiting our range of experiences and preventing us from finding fulfillment. But actually it is wrongdoing that destroys our freedom. If we orient our life toward the satisfaction of our own desires, our desires gain more and more of a grip on us, and our freedom diminishes.

The slide into slavery to sin often begins with very small infidelities and rejections of God's grace. Gradually abandoning prayer, little by little giving in to a bitter and cynical thought or feeling, step by step exposing ourselves to worldly influences and friends—all lead to the likelihood of ending up enslaved to sin. Small lies become a pattern of lying, and eventually we are liars. Small sexual sin leads to a pattern of sexual sin, and eventually we "can't help ourselves". We are promiscuous. The devil is patient and is content to begin with small infidelities, knowing that over a period of time bigger infidelities will follow.

On the other hand, if we grow in holiness, we experience greater freedom to love, to do what is right, to fulfill the purpose for which God has made us. Pope Paul VI gave a lively description of the freedom holiness brings when he spoke to a group of visitors about it:

> The true life,
> the life founded on truth, on love, on divine grace,
> the life of strong, austere, and joyful men who are
>   sustained by real ideas, by a transcendent
>   communion, which makes the spirit happy even
>   in the adversities of life,
> the life of the vocation of baptism, full of interior
>   song, which is not extinguished by death,
> the good, simple, honest, and serene life:
> Christian life.[1]

The Lord himself is the source of this inner freedom. The Apostle Paul writes:

> Now the Lord is the Spirit, and where the spirit of the Lord is, there is freedom. And we all, with

---

[1] Paul VI, General audience, November 23, 1977.

unveiled face, beholding the glory of the Lord, are being changed into his likeness from one degree of glory to another; for this comes from the Lord who is the Spirit (2 Cor 3:17–18).

Paul is referring to the spiritual freedom that enables us to enter God's presence as his sons and daughters. He is also alluding to the moral freedom to lead lives free of the influence of the world, the flesh, and the devil.

God Is at Work to Make Us Like Himself

We were created in the image of God. We have been disfigured by sin, but now the Spirit dwelling in us brings us more and more into conformity with Christ. It is an astonishing process. Here we are, going through our humdrum routines, and God is at work to make us like himself.

But notice that the process involves our looking to Christ, gazing on his beauty. It is God who is at work in us, but we must cooperate by seeking him, meditating on his word, praying, being mindful of him, desiring to know him more.

Paul also describes the process of being made like Christ in terms of "bearing the fruit of the Spirit". The fruit-bearing metaphor helps us understand the relationship between inner transformation and outward behavior. Full holiness is not a matter of right actions performed reluctantly, out of fear of God's punishment. While we should bear in mind the reality of God's punishment of sin, fear is not the mainspring of a deeply holy life. The inner principle of a holy life is the presence of God's Spirit in us. Holy living comes forth from a heart filled with the Holy Spirit, just as fruit grows on a tree that has the natural vitality sustained by good soil, sunshine, and water.

Before mentioning the fruit of the Spirit, Paul first writes of the opposite:

> But I say, walk by the Spirit, and do not gratify the desires of the flesh. For the desires of the flesh are against the Spirit, and the desires of the Spirit are against the flesh; for these are opposed to each other. . . . But if you are led by the Spirit you are not under the law. Now the works of the flesh are plain: fornication, impurity, licentiousness, idolatry, sorcery, enmity, strife, jealousy, anger, selfishness, dissension, party spirit, envy, drunkenness, carousing, and the like. I warn you, as I have warned you before, that those who do such things shall not inherit the kingdom of God! (Gal 5:16–17, 18–21).

By "the desires of the flesh" Paul means the inclinations of our fallen nature toward sin—and not just sexual sin, but every kind of sin. Indeed, Paul offers a surprising list of sins—different from the list we might draw up ourselves. He speaks not only of idolatry and sorcery and licentiousness—evils that we would easily recognize—but also bickering, selfish rivalries, and envy. *All* these kinds of conduct are manifestations of a life turned away from Christ. God wants us to put all this behavior to death, saying No to it by the power of the Spirit. As Paul says, "Those who do such things will not inherit the kingdom of God."

> But the fruit of the Spirit is love, joy, peace, patience, kindness, goodness, faithfulness, gentleness, self-control. . . . And those who belong to Christ Jesus have crucified the flesh with its passions and desires (Gal 5:22–23, 24).

The fruit is borne in our lives through the action of the Spirit, but we must cooperate. Paul urges us to *take hold* of the Spirit's help and *say No* to the desires of the flesh.

When he says "have crucified", he does not mean that the process is over. While we have died with Christ in baptism, there is a crucifying of sinful desires that must happen day by day. We have to put the nails in the coffin, as it were. This is one aspect of what it means to "deny ourselves", as Jesus calls us to do (Mt 16:24). When Jesus says to deny ourselves and take up our cross, he is telling us to deny our sinful desires to indulge in bickering, selfish rivalries, envy, and the rest of the cravings of the flesh.

Instead, we should say Yes to Christ, Yes to his love, his joy, his patience, his peace, which are near to us in his Spirit. We do not have to search high and low for these qualities of Christ; they are accessible to us in his Spirit, who lives in our hearts.

Saying No to our desires to lie, to indulge in illicit sexual pleasure, to speak against someone, or to steal something puts us in a stronger position for the Holy Spirit to work in us. We grow in virtue, righteousness, truthfulness, purity, and honesty. We need to do our part in denying our sinful tendencies by renouncing them and not acting on them. We need to ask for the Spirit's help to do this. Then the Holy Spirit can do his part transforming us, degree by degree and little by little, into the image of Christ.

We Need an Eternal Perspective on Life

As we grow in holiness and take on Christ's perspective for our lives, we become increasingly aware that life is short and that it is a preparation for eternity. The real question of overriding importance in our life becomes clearer and clearer—"What think ye of Jesus Christ?" Are we with him or against him? Are we living in his kingdom or according to the rule of his enemies? This, and not any other, is the truly great issue facing the human race. To die in the Lord is to make an incredible success of our lives, however little we may have achieved in the eyes of other people. To die unrepentant, no matter how successful we have been in other respects, is to end our lives in tragic failure. As we grow in holiness, this eternal perspective impresses itself on us more and more.

As we see the purpose of this life, we grow in our longing for heaven. Our consciousness of where we are headed increases. Paul gives us an insight into what God is preparing for us:

> For we know that if the earthly tent we live in [our human body] is destroyed, we have a building from God [our resurrected body], a house not made with hands, eternal in the heavens. Here indeed we groan, and long to put on our heavenly dwelling, so that by putting it on we may not be found naked. For while we are still in this tent, we sigh with anxiety; not that

we would be unclothed, but that we would be further clothed, so that what is mortal may be swallowed up by life. He who has prepared us for this very thing is God, who has given us the Spirit as a guarantee (2 Cor 5:1–5).

It is vital for us to know what we can have from God now, in this present life, so that we ask God for it. What we can have is the pledge of eternal life, the gift of God's own Spirit dwelling in us. But we also need to know where we are headed, what lies in the future, what we are being prepared for. It is literally our resurrection in Christ. Keeping the resurrection in view helps us live a holy life here and now. It gives us the motivation for holding on to what is good and persevering to the end. Paul follows his teaching about mortality being "absorbed by life" with a description of life lived from this perspective:

So we are always of good courage; we know that while we are at home in the body we are away from the Lord, for we walk by faith, not by sight. We are of good courage, and we would rather be away from the body and at home with the Lord. So whether we are at home or away, we make it our aim to please him. For we must all appear before the judgment seat of Christ, so that each one may receive good or evil, according to what he has done in the body (2 Cor 5:6–10).

In the New Testament we are cautioned to live our lives ready for judgment (Jas 2:12), preparing ourselves to give an account to God, mindful of the joy that is coming to us when Christ Jesus returns to judge the living and the dead

(1 Pet 1:6–7). As we grow in holiness, we grow in this mindfulness and joy.

When I face a decision in my own life or the life of my family, I regularly ask, "How will this affect our relationship in Christ? Will this weaken or increase my desire, our desire, to serve him? Will this help or hinder our decision to serve him, to grow in purity and holiness? Will this help us along the way to heaven, or will it be an assist on the way to hell?" There are only two destinations for all human beings ultimately—heaven or hell. We need to be mindful in which direction our decisions are leading us and our families.

We Are Being Prepared for Glory

Our lives are running out. Every passing moment carries us closer to death, closer to the loss of everything we have in this world. But in the larger perspective, we see that we are being prepared to live a better life. It is as though we are being expanded so that we will become capable of bearing a life full of glory, a life that would break us if it were given to us now. In our present passing life, the Holy Spirit is preparing us to bear this lasting life of glory.

Growing in holiness leads into a life that will truly satisfy. In the present world, we sometimes get what we want. It sometimes makes us happy, but it never brings us lasting satisfaction. We get a ticket to the World Series. We get a big house, a new car, even the children we wanted. But something in us asks, "Is that all there is?" Whatever it is, it is never enough. But that will not be the case with the kingdom of God. We will be satisfied with God's glory for eternity. Heaven will not disappoint.

The final phase of growth in holiness comes at death.

God holds our whole lives in his hands, including the timing and manner of our death. By arranging the circumstances of our life and our death, he unfolds his plan for us and brings his work in us to completion. He knows whether a quick death or a slow one is right for us, and he gives us what is best for us. To live well and die well is to live and die under his care, cooperating with his plan.

It is only when we die that God completes the process of our becoming holy. The Apostle John tells us:

> Beloved,
> we are God's children now;
> it does not yet appear what we shall be,
> but we know that when he appears
> we shall be like him,
> for we shall see him as he is.
> And everyone who thus hopes in him
> purifies himself as he is pure (1 Jn 3:2-3).

A final transformation will make us able to bear the weight of God's glory. The process of being made more and more like Christ will be completed, and we will be like him forever. In the twinkling of an eye, at the blast of the trumpet, what is mortal will be taken up and clothed with immortality, the perishable will become imperishable (1 Cor 15:52-55). God's plan for us will be fulfilled. We shall be holy as he is holy, and we shall see him as he is.

Because we have this hope, we follow him in this life and, by his grace, keep ourselves pure as he is pure.

8

The Means of Holiness

Having looked at the road to holiness, we can now examine some particular ways to make progress along the road.

We must keep in mind that while growth in holiness requires energetic cooperation on our part, holiness flows from God rather than from our own efforts. The key to growth is living each day in the fear and knowledge of the Lord, beholding his majesty, staying in his love. It is God's presence that transforms us. He lifts us from one degree of glory to the next as we look into the face of Christ (2 Cor 3:17–18).

It is not the things we do that make us holy, but God who makes us holy as we do the things he wants us to do. The means of holiness make us holy precisely because they help us to stay in contact with God. They keep our attention on him so we can remain open to the movements of his Spirit and fulfill his will for our lives. They help us stay near to the source of holiness, Jesus Christ.

At the very top of the list of the means of holiness is prayer. Books have been written about prayer, many of them helpful. But the important thing is not merely to know about prayer but to pray. Prayer is crucial! You may want to read more about prayer in my book *Hungry for God*.

I made the most important decision of my adult life on a retreat weekend as a senior at the University of Notre Dame. I came to the conclusion that God was right and I was wrong. I turned my life over to him. I took my position as a creature before the Creator. I got my priorities straight. The second most important decision followed immediately: I resolved to take time each day for personal prayer. I made those two decisions more than twenty years ago. Together they have revolutionized my life. Every passing year has given me a deeper conviction of the reality of Jesus Christ and the necessity of a daily time with him in personal prayer.

Make Time for Daily Personal Prayer
and Scripture Reading

My advice to anyone who is not taking any regular time every day to pray is *begin!* Start with ten or fifteen minutes a day. Increase the time you spend in prayer as your relationship with the Lord grows.

Basically, personal prayer is spending time before the Lord, pointing ourselves in his direction. Even if our mind is blank and we do not feel inspired or are not experiencing anything—even if we are tired or distracted— still, turning toward God lets him know we want him. It allows him to keep a hold on us, to keep his Spirit resting on us. Through regular prayer we begin to discern what is from him and what is not from him. If we have things we want to say in prayer, we can say them. If we do not have anything to say, we can at least sit and look to him. In the film version of Georges Bernanos' *Diary of a Country Priest*, an old priest gives a newly ordained priest some advice from his long experience. "At all costs, you must pray", he tells him. "And if you can't pray, just babble."

The natural accompaniment to prayer is Scripture reading. Think how much God has revealed to us in Scripture! How many of his purposes for human life! We need to avail ourselves of this revelation. Vital matters are explained to us in Scripture, matters on which our lives depend, matters of tremendous importance for the people around us. How foolish we are if we do not draw on the richness and wealth God offers us in Scripture.

I would make two recommendations about using the Scriptures. The first is to pray a few psalms each day, simply starting at the beginning of the Book of Psalms and going through the whole book. If we read five psalms every day, we can read the entire Psalter in one month. These prayers, which were inspired by the Holy Spirit, will form our prayer. These are prayers that Jesus prayed. They are prayers fulfilled in the New Testament. They can help us pray when we draw a blank and do not know what to say.

Second, choose one book of Scripture to read from beginning to end. Start with a short prayer asking God to speak to you and then read one chapter a day. Afterward, reflect on what you have read. Day by day we should be reading the Scriptures, exposing ourselves to God's word, letting it speak to us, making it the environment in which our minds grow. We will not have stupendous insights every day. But we will gradually grow in our knowledge of God and in our ability to see reality as he sees it.

Along with Scripture, we should make time for other spiritual reading, such as the lives of the saints. We should seek out books that heighten our desire for God and for holiness.

Help of a different kind comes to us through other people who want to take up their cross every day and follow the Lord. Contact with other members of the body of Christ is a source of strength for us. In a world that cares little about Christ, we need fellow Christians who can encourage us to follow him and who will call us on when we weaken or fall—rather than encourage us to give in to temptation!

Fellow disciples concerned for growing in holiness may take some seeking, but they are worth looking for. We might find them in our church, or in some evangelistic movement, or in some movement of spiritual renewal. If we don't seem to be able to find them, we should ask God to lead us to them.

Among such fellow disciples we would do well to find someone to whom we can hold ourselves accountable for conducting our lives in a righteous way and fulfilling our commitments to God and others. A Christian who is older and wiser and is able to play this role can be a source of counsel for us. Officially or unofficially this person can become a source of pastoral care, someone with whom we can share our lives and receive support and guidance. It is a shame to let pride or jealousy hold us back from availing ourselves of those whom God has placed in the body of Christ to help us along the way.

In a world where work is often tedious and ill rewarded, it is tempting to think that if only we could get away from the daily grind and have more time to pray and read Scripture, we could really zoom along the road to holiness. Our responsibilities can easily seem like obstacles to holiness.

But God, who wants to transform our entire lives, intends to transform us by using our entire lives. The particular means to holiness that we have been examining, while crucial, are not the only means through which God brings us to holiness. They are the irrigation channels that keep us open to the life-giving waters of the Spirit. The remainder of our lives are the fields where the waters soak into the ground and produce the harvest. Our duties to our families, our jobs, and so on are aspects of our lives where God wants us to be in contact with him. They are spheres of responsibility where God wants to be shaping us and making us like him. Time on the job or time spent doing housework is not time away from God; time spent in prayer is not the only time we are with God.

Our Work Can Be a Means to Holiness

The Letter to the Ephesians gives us instructions for approaching our work so as to grow in holiness:

Slaves, be obedient to those who are your earthly masters, with fear and trembling, in singleness of heart, as to Christ; not in the way of eye service, as men-pleasers, but as servants of Christ, doing the will of God from the heart, rendering service with a good will as to the Lord and not to men, knowing that whatever good one does, he will receive the same again from the Lord, whether he is a slave or free (Eph 6:5–8).

Even to slaves, who are giving forced labor, Paul brings the good news that they can work in a way that pleases the Lord. How much more we who do our work voluntarily!

Paul tells workers to serve with sincerity, putting in a good day's work, not simply marking time and doing as little as possible. Christ is pleased when we do a good job. Whether we are working in a factory or selling groceries or taking care of a home, our ordinary, mundane, seemingly unspiritual work is pleasing to God if we do it from the heart. He calls us to put ourselves into it, to work in a way that releases his power and grace into our lives.

As we work we should recall our identity. Paul reminds even slaves that they belong first to Christ rather than to men. As Christians we are sons and daughters of God, friends of Christ. We should seek to serve him rather than men. He is served when we do our jobs not simply to make a good impression but with the intention of pleasing him.

This can make an important difference in how we deal with frustrations and disappointments in our work. Often other people do not notice the good work we do. We may fail to get the promotions and raises we deserve. Our work in the home with our children may be unappreciated. But the Lord sees what we are doing. He sees if we are working sincerely and wholeheartedly, and he will reward us. We should not be working for our own advancement and enrichment or even, ultimately, for the support of those we are responsible for. No, we should do our work out of obedience to the Lord.

We will finally have to give him an account for all that we have done—not only for how we prayed but also for how we worked. He will examine whether we lived every day and performed all our work as an offering to him. Keeping that in mind can lift our spirits as we work and can help us cooperate in our work with God. He wants to use it to lead us along the road to holiness.

Thus our lives can be unified. The division of our days into different kinds of activities—into prayer and work, Scripture reading and changing diapers, sitting in church and sitting at a computer terminal—does not divide our lives into holy and unholy or spiritual and unspiritual categories. Our whole lives can be a way of serving Christ and growing holy. The very difficulties we encounter in our work become the instruments that God uses to uproot our self-seeking and self-gratification, our laziness and fear.

The challenges of our work create pressures that humble us, prodding us to relinquish our self-reliance and driving us closer to Christ for help. If we feel that we could better grow in holiness if only the problems and hardships of our work were removed, we are ignoring the fact that God often works through the aspects of our work that we find most distasteful. The very work that we find so unspiritual may be God's chosen means of helping us grow in unselfish love and service and abandonment to him.

Family Life Is the Road to Holiness
for Most of Us

What I have been saying is true in a special way of the responsibilities we have to the members of our families. Family life is the road to holiness that God has appointed for most of us. Family relationships are inherently a call to service. The terms *husband, wife, father, mother, son,* and *daughter* imply a responsibility to care.

In answering this call, we are responding to one of God's deepest invitations to holiness. Before addressing slaves, Paul spoke of this dimension of married love, comparing the relationship of husband and wife to the relationship of Christ and the Church:

> Wives, be subject to your husbands, as to the Lord. For the husband is the head of the wife as Christ is the head of the church, his body, and is himself its Savior. As the church is subject to Christ, so let wives also be subject in everything to their husbands. Husbands, love your wives, as Christ loved the church and gave himself up for her, that he might sanctify her, having cleansed her by the washing of water with the word, that he might present the church to himself in splendor, without spot or wrinkle or any such thing, that she might be holy and without blemish. Even so husbands should love their wives as their own bodies (Eph 5:22–28).

God's plan for marriage parallels his plan for mankind. As God sent his Son to purify a people for himself and bring them to holiness, so the husband is to love and serve his

wife so that she may grow in holiness. And as the husband
leads and cares for his wife, he becomes like Christ himself.
As the wife submits to her husband and cares for him, she is
submitting to the Lord, and thus she grows in holiness.

Paul goes on to remind children to honor—that is,
respect and obey—their parents "in the Lord". He also
reminds fathers to train and teach their children in a way
"befitting the Lord". In other words, both the sub-
missiveness and service that children give their parents and
the love and discipline that parents give their children are
to be given in a way that pleases the Lord through the
power that he provides. Thus these relationships are also a
means of growing in holiness.

Holiness for husbands and wives means being holy as
husbands and wives. It means loving and serving one
another. It means husbands caring for their wives. It means
wives submitting to their husbands. There is no way to
holiness for husbands and wives that bypasses holiness in
their relationships one to another. Holiness for children is
bound up in honoring, respecting, and obeying their parents. There is no way to holiness for children that bypasses
holiness in how they relate to their parents. Love and self-
denial in our primary relationships are necessary parts of
the way to holiness.

The Eucharist Can Be the Greatest Means
to Holiness

Finally, among the means of holiness, the union that Jesus
gives us with himself in the Eucharist is unique. Being a
Catholic, I believe that, in the Eucharist, the Lord gives

himself as our food to strengthen us for our journey along the road to holiness. Jesus said his Body is real food and his Blood real drink (Jn 6:28–65). In the Eucharist, he makes himself our nourishment on the way.

We have already considered the passage in 1 Corinthians in which Paul describes Jesus' institution of the Eucharist at the Last Supper and dwells on the holiness of Christ's presence in the bread and the cup. In the Eucharist we encounter God in all his holiness. The encounters of all the men and women of the Old Covenant with God are surpassed by the encounter we can have in the New Covenant with Christ (Lk 10:23–24).

The light and glory and dignity of the New Covenant infinitely surpass the Old Covenant (Lk 7:28; 2 Cor 3:7–11; Heb 1:1–4; 7:18–28). The place where we encounter Christ most intimately is in the gift of his Body and Blood. In the Eucharist his sacrifice on the Cross is made ever present to us. The New Covenant in his Blood is constantly renewed within us. His holy life is made ever available to us.

In the Eucharist we encounter the holy God making his home in the depth of our being. He freely shares his holiness with us, strengthening our union with himself and healing us of our selfishness. The Eucharist properly approached and responded to is thus the greatest means to holiness. It is for many the closest we ever come in this life to experiencing the union with God that lies at the end of the road to holiness that we are traveling. There are many helpful books on the Eucharist. One that presents the Catholic perspective well is *Eucharist* by Louis Bouyer.[1]

---

[1] Louis Bouyer, *Eucharist* (South Bend, Ind.: University of Notre Dame Press, 1968).

9

God's Part and Ours

Have you ever heard the advice "Let go and let God"? Or "Pray as though everything depends on God and work as though everything depends on yourself"? What about the expression "Praise the Lord and pass the ammunition"?

All three statements touch on a question that arises in the process of growing in holiness: How much does God do, and how much do we do? To what extent is the process up to God, and to what extent is it up to us? This is not merely a question that theologians might speculate about. It affects our lives day by day. Should I stop striving to get a particular problem solved and "let God" do it? Will a weakness in my life get straightened out through more faith or more hard work?

There are no stock answers to such questions. Each situation has to be examined carefully. But it is possible to clear up a couple of misconceptions that sometimes cloud our thinking.

On the one hand, we can slip into thinking that we get

holy by our own efforts. Having been humbled by the holiness of God and having repented of our sins, we may get up from our knees and go off and try to live a holy life pretty much on our own steam. "Thank you, Lord, for saving me from my sins. I'll take it from here." By ourselves we plan to stop doing what is wrong and start doing what is right. We think we can simply use the various means of growing holy and show God just how good we can be!

Or we may avoid this approach of being independent by sitting back and waiting for God to act. Holiness comes from God, not from us, right? So let God do it. "I'm just a sinner, trusting in his mercy. If he wants me to change, it's up to him."

The first approach is obviously mistaken. It leaves God out of the picture, and there is no holiness apart from him. He is the fountain of all holiness. Christ came into the world so that we could share in his holiness, and we must be united to him in order to receive his holiness. Branches can grow only when they are connected to the trunk of the plant to which they belong. The trunk is the source of their common life. The Apostle John uses this analogy to help us understand how we must be united to Christ to have a share in his life, a share in his holiness (see Jn 15:1–6).

The second approach seems more spiritual, but it too is mistaken. It assumes that there is only so much effort that can go into making us holy, and we can maximize God's input by minimizing our own. In this view, growing in holiness is pictured somewhat like two people buying a piece of property. The property has a set market value, say

$100,000, and the more money the first person puts toward the purchase, the less the second does; the more money the second person puts up, the less the first does. Applying this model to growth in holiness, some people think that the more effort they put in, the less God can contribute. Wanting God to do a lot, they decide to do hardly anything.

God's Grace and Our Efforts Work Together

A better analogy for growing in holiness is the relation between a political candidate and his financial backers. There is no fixed limit to the amount of money the politician can use. If he has $10,000, he can mount a small campaign. If he has $1 million, he can hire a staff and put on a big campaign. There is no conflict or competition between his efforts and those of his financial supporters.

The two kinds of effort are different. The harder he works at campaigning, the more effectively he will be able to use his supporters' contributions to bring his message to the voters. We might think of ourselves as the politician and God as our "backer". When it comes to growing in holiness, our efforts do not replace God's help. Neither does his help replace our efforts. The harder we work at cooperating with God's "support", the more we grow in his likeness.

God's grace and our efforts, although very different from each other, are supposed to work together. We inevitably wander off the road to holiness if we set God's grace and our efforts in opposition to each other. The Christian life is grace from beginning to end—an undeserved gift from a merciful God. But it is not a gift for us to receive passively. The gift is given so that we will be able to fulfill the purpose for which God made us but that we were unable to fulfill without his help.

He made us to *know*, *love*, and *serve* him in this world and to be with him forever in the next. By his grace he makes us able to fulfill our destiny in Christ. The gift of his life comes to lift us up out of the quicksand of our sins and weaknesses, to put us on solid ground, and to make us able to serve him.

We enter this life of holiness not through doing anything good that attracts God or makes us deserving of his love. We enter only by his act of compassion and mercy in Christ. We simply take hold of what he has done for us:

> Since we are justified by faith, we have peace with God through our Lord Jesus Christ (Rom 5:1).

It is faith—believing in what God has provided for us— that saves us. We do not save ourselves by becoming holy and then saying to God, "Now am I holy enough for you to save me?" We cannot become holy on our own efforts. God has to do something radical in us to make us able to obey him. Our part is to believe in the salvation he has given us in the death and Resurrection of Jesus.

But faith and obedience go together, too. Belief in Christ cannot be separated from obedience. That is why Paul speaks of leading the nations to "obedient faith" (Rom 1:5). And this obedience, in turn, cannot be separated from God's grace because both the desire and ability to obey are given by God:

> For God is at work in you, both to will and to work
> for his good pleasure (Phil 2:13).

Or, as another translation says, "any measure of willing or doing". God gives us the grace to will and to do what pleases him. He gives us the grace to believe and obey when we first encounter his holiness, hear the gospel, and are converted. And he gives us the grace to believe and obey him day by day as he transforms us from one degree of glory to the next:

> And I am sure that he who began a good work in you
> will bring it to completion at the day of Jesus Christ
> (Phil 1:6).

God Gives Us the Grace and Strength We Need

Having claimed us as his own, Jesus does not abandon us and leave us orphans (Jn 14:18). He does not save us only to send us out to become holy by ourselves. He is with us and in us, working to give us the power to say No when we need to and to say Yes when we need to. He lives in us, giving us the power to endure what we have to endure, to resist what we have to resist, to run the race and fight the good fight:

> For I through the law died to the law, that I might
> live to God. I have been crucified with Christ; it is no
> longer I who live, but Christ who lives in me; and the
> life I now live in the flesh I live by faith in the Son of
> God, who loved me and gave himself for me (Gal
> 2:19–20).

Elsewhere Scripture says that we have been purchased with a price and do not belong to ourselves anymore; we belong to Christ (1 Cor 6:19–20). He lives in us. Living in us, he is our "hope of glory" (Col 1:27). We still live our human lives, but now by faith we have been reunited to the source of our lives, the Son of God, who has loved us and has given himself for us.

God's grace is powerful, and it gives us the power to make a vigorous response. The life that Scripture talks about does not consist of intellectual belief only. It is a response of our whole being to God—mind, heart, and strength (see Mk 12:30). Faith is obedient reliance and trust, not disobedient passivity and presumption. It is not saying "I believe" and then not doing anything about it (Jas 2:14–26). Jesus says, "If you love me, obey my commandments" (Jn 14:21). He gives us the power to do just that. The Holy Spirit is at work within us to make our faith active rather than passive, obedient rather than presumptuous.

Scripture repeatedly summons us to strong, whole-hearted cooperation with God's grace:

> Let not sin therefore reign in your mortal bodies, to make you obey their passions. Do not yield your members to sin as instruments for wickedness, but yield yourselves to God as men who have been brought from death to life, and your members to God as instruments of righteousness. For sin will have no dominion over you, since you are not under the law but under grace (Rom 6:12–14).

In Christ we have freely been given the power to say No to sin. We should *use* it! God has graciously equipped us for holy living. We should stop using our bodies to sin and should offer ourselves to God. Scripture bears witness that it is God who does everything in us. And in passage after passage it calls us to make a vigorous response:

> If your right eye causes you to sin, *pluck it out and throw it away*; it is better that you lose one of your members than that your whole body be thrown into hell. And if your right hand causes you to sin, *cut it off and throw it away*; it is better that you lose one of your members than that your whole body go into hell (Mt 5:29–30).

> *Shun* immorality. Every other sin which a man commits is outside the body; but the immoral man sins against his own body. Do you not know that your body is a temple of the Holy Spirit within you, which you have from God? You are not your own; you were bought with a price. So *glorify* God in your body (I Cor 6:18–20).

> *Strive* for peace with all men, and for the holiness without which no one will see the Lord. *See to it* that no one fail to obtain the grace of God; that no "root of bitterness" spring up and cause trouble, and by it the many become defiled. . . . See that you *do not refuse* him who is speaking (Heb 12:14–15, 25).

Sometimes We Need to Take Radical Action

God's grace enables us to take radical action when radical action needs to be taken, both to do good and to turn from evil. Holiness is something that God does in us and gives to us; it is also something that his grace enables us to maintain and to grow in. He expects us to regard highly the holiness that he has placed in our life, to regard highly our new status as temples of the Holy Spirit and members of Christ's body. And his grace is with us imparting power to us to strive for holiness, to desire closeness to him, to desire purity of heart.

I know many people who, in order to be free from sin, needed to decide not to associate with certain people, not to frequent certain places, not to listen to certain music, not to read certain magazines, not to see certain movies. Not until they prayerfully identified what was leading them to sin and took definite action to break with those occasions of sin did they begin to make real progress in getting free. Some people I have known have literally left their native land or their town to avail themselves of Christian support. They literally needed a change in environment to remain free from sin.

"See that you do not refuse him who is speaking." We face choices all along the way. But God's grace is with us now to enable us to hear him when he speaks and to overcome temptation and the tendencies of the flesh.

> Since we have these promises, beloved, let us cleanse ourselves from every defilement of body and spirit, and make holiness perfect in the fear of God (2 Cor 7:1).

Certainly it is God who purifies us, but Scripture speaks of our taking action too: "Let us cleanse ourselves." Let us take action to remove from our lives those things that are impure and to turn toward the purity of Christ. The Holy Spirit makes it possible for us to do this, but we must act ourselves.

Exhortations to us to work actively with God's grace appear throughout the New Testament:

Submit yourselves therefore to God. *Resist* the devil and he will flee from you. *Draw near* to God, and he will draw near to you. *Cleanse* your hands, you sinners, and *purify* your hearts, you men of double mind. . . . Humble yourselves before the Lord and he will exalt you (Jas 4:7–8, 10).

We can submit to God and obey him. We can resist the devil because the Holy Spirit has been given to us.

Fight the good fight of the faith; *take hold* of the eternal life to which you were called (1 Tim 6:12).

Again, we can fight because the Holy Spirit has been poured into our hearts.

Do you not know that in a race all the runners compete, but only one receives the prize? So *run* that you may obtain it. Every athlete exercises self-control in all things. They do it to receive a perishable wreath, but we an imperishable (1 Cor 9:24–25).

Let us also lay aside every weight, and sin which clings so closely, and let us run with perseverance the race that is set before us (Heb 12:1).

Growing in holiness does not mean sitting back and taking it easy. It means going for the gold! God wants us to order our lives to reach the goal. Athletes deny themselves all sorts of things. Self-denial is important for the Christian, too (Lk 9:23). But self-denial is not the force that enables us to run; the Spirit enables us. We should run not from our own strength, but we should be swept forward by the Spirit of God, who is enabling us to run the race and to fight the good fight.

> *Stir into flame* the gift of God (2 Tim 1:6 NAB, italics added).

A great gift has been given to us—the very life of God. We are not to be passive receptacles of it but willing subjects, receiving it, stirring it up, valuing it, acting on it, moving on in the power of God.

10

Holiness and Love

Paul's Letter to the Ephesians leads off with a tremendous hymn of praise and thanksgiving. Paul was excited at the greatness of God's love, especially at the fact that God had us in mind from all eternity. We are not an afterthought of God or an accident in the universe that he is now claiming for his own in Christ. As Paul praises God, he teaches us something important about holiness:

> Praised be the God and Father of our Lord Jesus Christ, who has bestowed on us in Christ every spiritual blessing in the heavens! God chose us in him before the world began, to be holy and blameless in his sight, to be full of love; he likewise predestined us through Christ Jesus to be his adopted sons—such was his will and pleasure (Eph 1:3–5 NAB).

"Holy and blameless" and our destiny "to be full of love" are really two different ways of talking about the same thing. To be holy is to be filled with love, to be "in love" with God. Sin—uncleanness and unholiness—creates a blockage to love. Sin, the opposite of holiness, is selfish-ness, the opposite of love. To be unholy is to be unloving. To be holy is to love.

Sometimes when we talk about great holiness, images come to mind of great self-denial, of rigorous penance and turning to the Lord. We might picture a monk fasting in his monastery. Certainly that can be a path to holiness. But if the monk is truly embracing external austerities in the Holy Spirit, they are producing a heart open ever wider to love, a man more able to say No to self and Yes to God, to pour himself out in prayer and service for his brethren and for the whole world.

To become holy is to become loving. That is why Scripture sometimes phrases the call to holiness in terms of love. Jesus taught on one occasion that we should "be perfect as our Father in heaven is perfect" (Mt 5:48). On another occasion he taught that we must love with all our being. The first commandment, he said, is:

> You shall love the Lord your God with all your heart, and with all your soul, and with all your mind, and with all your strength (Mk 12:30).

The second commandment, he said, is like the first:

> You shall love your neighbor as yourself (Mk 12:31).

The call to holiness is a call to love completely with everything we are and everything we have, to love God and to love our fellow men with our whole being.

Jesus returned to this teaching at the end of his life, as a kind of last will and testament to his followers. Just before he was arrested and crucified he told them:

A new commandment I give to you, that you love one another; even as I have loved you, that you also love one another. . . . As the Father has loved me, so have I loved you; abide in my love (Jn 13:34; 15:9).

God is inviting us to share in his own love, to partake of the love that is being poured out between the Father and the Son and the Holy Spirit. We are being called into the life of the Holy Trinity. We should let the love that is flowing between the Father and the Son and the Holy Spirit catch us up. We should let it purify us, form us, and manifest itself through us.

Paul speaks of this same reality when he writes about the gift of the Spirit to those who are in Christ:

Hope does not disappoint us, because God's love has been poured into our hearts through the Holy Spirit which has been given to us (Rom 5:5).

One of the greatest biblical passages on holiness does not actually use the word *holiness* at all but speaks entirely in terms of love. It is the famous description of love in 1 Corinthians 13, which is likewise a picture of holiness.

If I speak in the tongues of men and of angels, but have not love, I am a noisy gong or a clanging cymbal. And if I have prophetic powers, and understand all mysteries and all knowledge, and if I have all faith, so as to remove mountains, but have not love, I am nothing. If I give away all I have, and if I deliver my body to be burned, but have not love, I gain nothing. Love is patient and kind (1 Cor 13:1–4).

Paul is talking about the fruit of the Spirit (Gal 5:22–23). He is talking about the character of God, which God wants to form in our lives by the Holy Spirit.

> Love is not jealous or boastful; it is not arrogant or rude. Love does not insist on its own way; it is not irritable or resentful; it does not rejoice at wrong, but rejoices in the right. Love bears all things, believes all things, hopes all things, endures all things.

> Love never ends; as for prophecies, they will pass away; as for tongues, they will cease; as for knowledge, it will pass away. For our knowledge is imperfect and our prophecy is imperfect; but when the perfect comes, the imperfect will pass away. When I was a child, I spoke like a child, I thought like a child, I reasoned like a child; when I became a man I gave up childish ways. For now we see in a mirror dimly, but then face to face. Now I know in part; then I shall understand fully, even as I have been fully understood. So faith, hope, love abide, these three; but the greatest of these is love (1 Cor 13:4–13).

Growing in Holiness Means Growing in Love

One of the important ways of growing in holiness is looking to see whom God has placed us in relationship with to love, and then loving them as Christ loves us. The road to holiness leads us to serve our families, our friends, our relatives, our neighbors, our coworkers—the people God has put us with in our daily lives.

A sign of growth in holiness for many men has meant

deciding to take responsibility for their wives and children. A sign of growth in holiness for many women has meant forgiving their husbands for past failings and seeking to serve them in Christian love. A sign of growth in holiness for those who are in difficult work situations has meant not simply reacting to coworkers and their problems but really praying for them and seeking to relate properly to them.

As we grow in holiness, we will be less likely to take offense and more likely to be the one who bridges the gap when there is tension and pressure in relationships. We will be less likely to fall into dissension and rivalry. We will be more able to hang in there, loving when things get difficult.

"Love believes all things, love bears all things, love endures all things, love hopes all things." That is the love of Christ. And as we grow in holiness and the love of Christ grows in us, we become more capable of being the one who goes more than halfway for others, the one who forgives again and again. We become more able to love even when we are not being loved in return, to give even when we are not receiving anything back. As the famous Christian mystic John of the Cross says, "Where there is no love pour in love, and you shall draw out love." We become more capable of acting out of compassion when we notice opportunities for doing good that are not strictly our responsibility.

Francis of Assisi asked God to give him this kind of holiness in his famous prayer:

Lord, make me an instrument of your peace.
Where there is hatred, let me sow love,

where there is injury, pardon,
where there is doubt, faith,
where there is despair, hope,
where there is darkness, light,
where there is sadness, joy.
O Divine Master, grant that I may not so much seek
    to be consoled as to console,
to be understood as to understand,
to be loved as to love,
for it is in giving that we receive,
it is in pardoning that we are pardoned,
it is in dying that we are born to eternal life.

Scripture says God has prepared us to walk in good works (Eph 2:10). He has placed people in our path whom we can serve with a word of truth or a deed of kindness. He has put resources in our hands that we can use to show mercy to people and to extend the kingdom of God. As we grow in holiness, we grow in love. We become more able to live as Jesus lived, giving without counting the cost, without receiving in return, taking our joy in being sustained and nourished by doing the will of our Father in heaven (Jn 4:31–34). God is holy. God is love. As we grow in holiness, we are to grow in love for God and our fellow men.

I I

Holiness and Suffering

Margie, a friend of mine, was in an auto accident a few years ago. The main injury she suffered was to her right knee, which was smashed. As soon as the swelling went down, doctors performed surgery on the knee and put her leg in a cast. The surgery was more painful than the accident itself, and for a few days the doctors prescribed some serious painkilling medication. Then for three months her condition stabilized. The pain eased, and she could get around a little in her cast.

But Margie was less than halfway to recovery. The day came when the cast was taken off, which felt good to her but was followed by some of the most difficult days of her life. During the time she was wearing the cast, her leg muscles had stiffened, contracted, and weakened. Now she could hardly move her leg at all—and what little she could do hurt. The only way for her to regain full use of her leg was to undergo painful physical therapy and grueling exercises. Margie showed her grit.

The fact that today Margie can run and ride a bike is a testimony to God's grace, her physical therapist's skill, and her own perseverance.

Margie's experience of recovery is similar to our growing in holiness. When we go astray from God and his will for our lives, we suffer various injuries of the spirit. The first step toward wholeness is turning to Christ. His forgiveness might be compared to Margie's surgery. In one sense, everything is set right at this point. We are reconciled to God. But in another sense, we have a long way to go. Just as Margie could not immediately stand up and walk out of the operating room, neither can we immediately live a life of love, mercy, faithfulness, joy, service—a life marked by all the fruit of the Spirit.

Like Margie, we eventually have to face the aspects of our personalities that are not whole. The casts are removed, and we find that we are still crippled, stunted persons. Christ has taken away our guilt; but as a result of our own sins and others' sins against us our hearts are still stony, our minds worldly, our emotions disordered. The process of becoming holy, therefore, must be a process of rehabilitation. We have been received into God's kingdom. But we are in the rehabilitation section—the Church on earth.

Our twistedness and stoniness need to be straightened out and melted by God's love. We might say we have to be "kneaded" by the Holy Spirit, the way a physical therapist massages contracted muscles. Our hearts have a small capacity for love. Our minds have a small ability to understand. We need stretching so that we can live God's life fully.

Sometimes we require vigorous kneading, kneading that hurts. Some of the exercises to enlarge our spiritual range of motion may be excruciating.

Margie would sometimes say to the therapist, "That hurts. Isn't there some other way to get these muscles working?" And she would be tempted to say, "I'd prefer to leave it. I can't stretch out my leg all the way, but I'll just live with it as it is. I can't stand any more of this pushing and pulling."

God knows our limits. He knows how much kneading and stretching and exercising we can take. He is not going to break us. But he is serious about straightening out the stunted, withered, twisted aspects of our being. There is no denying that often the process hurts. But there is no path to the joy of loving that does not lead through the painfulness of being straightened and enlarged.

To Become Holy, We Must Die to Ourselves

Holiness and suffering are connected. And the reason holiness sometimes hurts is not that there is anything alien and unnatural about it. The process of becoming holy hurts primarily because there is so much resistance to be overcome in ourselves before we are able to live the holy life that God has designed us for.

Jesus explicitly told his disciples to expect that following him would entail suffering:

> If any man would come after me, let him deny himself and take up his cross and follow me. For whoever would save his life will lose it, and whoever loses his life for my sake will find it (Mt 16:24–25).

What kind of self-denial is Jesus speaking about? Some of it is internal self-denial—saying No to the twisted, bent, shriveled tendencies of our fallen nature and Yes to the straightening-out process. We experience the pain of saying No to temptations that may really attract us—things like lying, stealing, and impurity. We also experience pain in saying Yes when the Spirit prompts us to express love, praise of God, humble service, generous giving, and loyalty in new and uncomfortable ways. There are times too when we would simply "rather not".

In denying ourselves, the pain of emptiness comes before the joy of filling. We cannot be fulfilled unless we are filled with God, and we cannot be filled with God unless we are first emptied of sin.

Self-denial also means the pain of saying No to the world, insofar as the world is organized against the kingdom of God. Paul writes:

> But far be it from me to glory except in the cross of our Lord Jesus Christ, by which the world has been crucified to me, and I to the world (Gal 6:14).

We must recognize that we no longer belong to the world in the sense of having any obligation to live in ways that people commend but God detests. Jesus tells us that we need to be *in* the world but not *of* it, in it but not belonging to it. We are in the world as children of God and as servants of Christ. But we belong to the new heaven and the new earth that is coming, not to the present world, the form of which is temporary and passing away (1 Cor 7:31).

As Christians our proper relationship to the world

is summed up in a statement in the First Epistle of John:

> In this is love perfected with us, that we may have confidence for the day of judgment, because as he is so are we in this world (1 Jn 4:17).

In other words, our way of dealing with this world should be just like Jesus' way. He loved the world in the sense that he thanked his Father for creating the universe and providing for his creatures. He loved it in the sense that he loved all men and women.

But Jesus did not love the world in the sense of having his focus on this life or in the sense of compromising with the deceptions and temptations that lead people astray from God's purposes. Jesus declared, "My kingdom is not of this world" (Jn 18:36 NAB). His purpose in coming into this world was not to enjoy himself or to amass a fortune or to make a big impression on people or to lead a quiet life free from trouble (see Mt 4:1–11). He was here as a servant. He was here to lay down his life as a sacrifice for sin, as a ransom for many (Mt 20:28). He washed his disciples' feet. He spoke the truth in love. He healed people and set them free. He delivered them from the bondages of evil and sin and sickness. John tells us that we can have confidence on the day of judgment if our relationship to the world becomes just like Jesus' relationship to it.

Another aspect of self-denial consists in relinquishing our desires and expectations—even good ones—when God allows circumstances to remove from us things we want to have.

God allows us to encounter difficulties, adversities, persecution. These are the consequences of living in a world that has turned its back on God and is pervaded with evil spirits. The difficulties or adversities or persecutions are contrary to God's original plan for mankind, but they are not beyond his control. God is sovereign, and nothing happens to us except the good things that he directly intends or the evil things that he permits.

God Turns to Good the Evil in Our Lives

If God permits evil to happen to us, it is for the advancement of his kingdom in us and through us. *God allows evil to come into our lives only because he has a plan for turning the tables on the devil and defeating him through our response to those difficulties.* If we respond in a spirit of self-denial, trusting God and enduring patiently, God works in us and through us to accomplish his purposes.

If we think about it, this is good news. It means that the problems and hardships we have to deal with are tools in God's hands for making us holy. This was Paul's point when he wrote to the Romans:

> We know that in everything God works for good with those who love him, who are called according to his purpose (Rom 8:28).

God works in us with sufficient strength to accomplish his objectives. He knows what needs to be purified in us and how much force needs to be applied. If there is great hardness in our heart, some heavy blows may have to fall for that hardness to be broken.

This is not as strange an idea as it might seem at first. Parents realize that serious problems may require serious remedies. They know that to avoid serious remedies when they are needed is hardly loving. There is even a national movement, called the Tough Love Society, of parents whose children are rebellious or use drugs. These parents have learned the uselessness of wishy-washy dialogue or feckless affirmation ("Whatever is meaningful to you, Son, is fine with me"). They have discovered that sometimes a young person needs tough love ("Son, if you're going to continue to destroy yourself with drugs, you can't live in my house").

God's love is tough. His love is effective: it accomplishes its purpose. C. S. Lewis called it "severe mercy". God is merciful toward us, and it is an effective mercy, a mercy powerful enough to set us free, to break through our resistances and bring us into freedom.

For some of us, our hardness and stuntedness consist in self-reliance—a refusal to lean on God. In others it is an independent streak—an unwillingness to submit to authority of any kind. Or it is a reluctance to take responsibility for other people; or an absorption with ourselves. Some of us have attachments to comforts, or sex, or money. God may allow any number of difficulties or misfortunes to befall us to break through our stubbornness, to show us the emptiness and insufficiency of our approach to life, to bring us to the point of repentance. Sickness may play a role, or failure, or disappointment by those we love.

Although God's mercy may sometimes seem severe, we can completely entrust ourselves to his care for us.

His love for us is pure, without any harshness or vindictiveness. He will use difficulties to bring us to holiness, but he will never let them crush us if we stay in his grace and look to him for help. Paul tells us:

> God is faithful, and he will not let you be tempted beyond your strength, but with the temptation will also provide the way of escape, that you may be able to endure it (1 Cor 10:13).

In his loving wisdom and power, God measures the suffering he allows to come our way. He stands beside us ready to give us help.

At times it is hard to remember this. We find ourselves hard-pressed, tested to our limits. Perhaps we suffer in family relationships, or in business dealings, or in lawsuits, or in the death of those near to us, or in the handicaps and sicknesses of our children, or in loneliness, or in the pain of being faithful despite the unfaithfulness of our spouse. We may suffer sickness, unemployment, injustices, ostracism, mockery, or being misunderstood. At such times we can have the assurance that God is allowing our suffering and is with us in it. We can be assured that he is working holiness and love into our lives through it. His hand is on us. He is able to protect us from everything we need protection from, and he permits only that which should be allowed for our good and his glory.

Suffering Can Make Us Truly Wise

All suffering can work to produce a clear understanding of what is important. It can help us keep our priorities clear.

It can produce confidence in God rather than in ourselves, humbling us, showing us our limits and weaknesses, convincing us of how much we need power from on high and help from God. Thus suffering can make us truly wise. I know in my own life I am never so aware of my need for God, never so aware of my own limitations, never so appreciative of all the gifts of God than when I am sick.

It should be encouraging for us to know that even Jesus as a man grew through suffering:

> Although he was a Son, he learned obedience through what he suffered; and being made perfect he became the source of eternal salvation to all who obey him (Heb 5:8–9).

Even Jesus gained something in the human maturity of his holiness through the suffering the Father allowed him to undergo.

Whatever it is in us that needs to be straightened and enlarged, and whatever means God brings to bear, the best thing we can do is turn ourselves in, so to speak, and surrender to God. It is quicker and less painful in the long run to cooperate with God than to resist him. When we submit to him we discover how merciful he is. He is the physician of our souls. He knows how to touch things in us, how to straighten things out in us. Like the patient on the operating table, we do better not to squirm under the surgeon's knife but to hold still.

We might as well come to terms with the fact that, while God works some changes in our lives easily and peacefully, trials and difficulties play an essential role in the accomplishment of his plans for us. The triumph of Christ

in us, the overcoming of evil, our growth in holiness and
love—these can be achieved only through some degree of
hardship and difficulty.

Because this is so, the New Testament writers often
urge us to accept trials and recognize the positive work
that God will accomplish through them. In one passage
Paul explains that salvation comes to us from God through
Christ at his initiative, and we need merely open our
hearts in faith to receive it. But, he goes on to tell us, the
way we choose to deal with hardships plays an important
role in our growth in holiness:

> Therefore, since we are justified by faith, we have
> peace with God through our Lord Jesus Christ.
> Through him we have obtained access to this grace in
> which we stand, and we rejoice in our hope of
> sharing the glory of God. More than that, we rejoice
> in our sufferings, knowing that suffering produces
> endurance, and endurance produces character, and
> character produces hope, and hope does not disap-
> point us, because God's love has been poured into
> our hearts through the Holy Spirit which has been
> given to us (Rom 5:1–5).

We are being shown the secrets of soul surgery in this
passage, the secrets of how God works with human beings. And we can observe a certain logic: affliction makes
for endurance; endurance makes for tested virtue. Without
testing, what is virtue? It is easy to be virtuous if we are
not tempted to do wrong. It is easy not to steal if we feel
no inclination to steal. It is only under testing that we
discover whether we are honest. And, Paul continues,

tested virtue makes for hope. The more we see God building his strength into us, the more hope we have of our destiny: to come before Christ's judgment seat without being ashamed at how our life has gone. Thus, the more we can look forward to his return in glory.

We Need to See God's Purpose in Suffering

James was another apostle who saw the purpose of trials so clearly that he could rejoice when they came:

> Count it all joy, my brethren, when you meet various trials, for you know that the testing of your faith produces steadfastness. And let steadfastness have its full effect, that you may be perfect and complete, lacking in nothing (Jas 1:2–4).

They knew something, these first Christians. They understood what God is doing in our life when he sends us trials. As a result, the early Christians were everywhere characterized by joy. Whether, like Paul, they traveled widely or, like James, they stayed at home—they grasped the same truth about God's action through suffering to make us holy. It is an insight that God wants us to grasp today.

As Jesus and the apostles speak of the hardships we encounter on the road to holiness, they constantly remind us of the goal we are moving toward. They encourage us with the vision of what lies ahead. They are realistic about both the difficulties of the process and the splendor of the outcome. Jesus told his disciples:

> There is no one who has left house or brothers or
> sisters or mother or father or children or lands, for
> my sake and for the gospel, who will not receive a
> hundredfold now in this time, houses and brothers
> and sisters and mothers and children and lands, with
> persecutions, and in the age to come eternal life (Mk
> 10:29–30).

Persecutions and troubles of all kinds we will always have. But God will give us others who are also following him to support us. We should look around us to see who the fellow Christians might be with whom God is calling us to such a relationship. It helps to build these relationships before we need them.

Jesus not only warns us of persecutions and assures us of his help, but he also turns our attention to the age to come, to eternal life. Our present life is always going to have its sorrows and difficulties. And while we will receive some rewards in this life, the greatest reward is coming only at Christ's return. Then there will be no more sorrow or tears or death, and God will be all in all, everything to everybody (Rev 21:4; 1 Cor 15:28).

Paul likewise points us to this fulfillment, by speaking of us as heirs of God. Heirs naturally look forward to receiving their inheritance:

> For all who are led by the Spirit of God are sons of
> God. For you did not receive the spirit of slavery to
> fall back into fear, but you have received the spirit of
> sonship. When we cry, "Abba! Father!" it is the Spirit
> himself bearing witness with our spirit that we are
> children of God, and if children, then heirs, heirs of

God and fellow heirs with Christ, provided we suffer with him in order that we may also be glorified with him (Rom 8:14–17).

We are going to inherit everything that is waiting for Christ—the whole universe, new heavens and a new earth. We are going to reign with Christ. Realizing that we have a share in this inheritance should strengthen us as we suffer with him.

We Have a Share in the Sufferings of Christ

The idea of suffering with Christ is a mystery that goes beyond what we can understand. Jesus' death was more than adequate for taking away the sins of all the world. But in some way we are called to walk as he walked. In our own small way, in our own lives, we are called to "make up in our bodies what is lacking in the sufferings of Christ" (Col 1:24 NAB). God is giving us the blessing of being able to share in the sufferings of Christ as a way of making even more meaningful our participation in his glory. In a way this participation helps extend to the world the redemption that he brought with his death on the Cross.

Finally, let us consider the great passage in the Letter to the Hebrews that sums up so much of what we have been considering about suffering and holiness:

Therefore, since we are surrounded by so great a cloud of witnesses, let us also lay aside every weight, and sin which clings so closely (Heb 12:1).

The witnesses are the angels and the saints, who have demonstrated, by word and deed, their faith in Jesus. They are cheering us on as we strive for holiness, praying for us, interceding for us with Jesus, who is himself at the right hand of the Father interceding for us (Heb 7:25).

> And let us run with perseverance the race that is set before us, looking to Jesus the pioneer and perfecter of our faith (Heb 12:1–2).

In other words, let us keep the goal in view and not forget why we are doing what we are doing.

> For the joy that was set before him [he] endured the cross, despising the shame, and is seated at the right hand of the throne of God. Consider him who endured from sinners such hostility (Heb 12:2-3).

Thus Jesus himself is an example of keeping the goal in view

> so that you may not grow weary or fainthearted. In your struggle against sin you have not yet resisted to the point of shedding your blood. And have you forgotten the exhortation which addresses you as sons? "My son, do not regard lightly the discipline of the Lord, nor lose courage when you are punished by him. For the Lord disciplines him whom he loves" (Heb 12:3–6).

Good parents sometimes practice tough love, and so does God. It is precisely *because* we love our children that we discipline them. We do not want them to grow up to be lazy, good-for-nothing, self-centered, miserable, frustrated people. We train them, we teach them, we punish them, so that eventually they can share in the joy and happiness of maturity. That is how God loves us. But he is training and disciplining us for lasting things—to share in his holiness and bear the weight of his glory (see Rom 8:18).

> It is for discipline that you have to endure. God is treating you as sons; for what son is there whom his father does not discipline? If you are left without discipline, in which all have participated, then you are illegitimate children and not sons. Besides this, we have had earthly fathers to discipline us and we respected them. Shall we not much more be subject to the Father of spirits and live? For they disciplined us for a short time at their pleasure, but he disciplines us for our good, that we may share his holiness. For the moment all discipline seems painful rather than pleasant; later it yields the peaceful fruit of righteousness to those who have been trained by it. Therefore lift your drooping hands and strengthen your weak knees, and make straight paths for your feet, so that what is lame may not be put out of joint but rather be healed (Heb 12:7–13).

The process of having our limbs straightened, our knees strengthened, our hearts enlarged is painful at times. All discipline hurts; the writer of Hebrews admits that. But thereby God kneads his holiness into us and prepares us to see him. Then, when our whole being is flooded with the light and joy of his presence, every difficulty along the way will be seen to have played only the part that God intended it to play in opening our hearts wide to receive his love forever. Then, the suffering of the present age will truly be seen as nothing compared to the weight of glory rushing in on us as we meet Jesus face to face. Let none of us, then, receive the grace of God in vain, but let us dedicate ourselves to striving for that "holiness without which no one will see the Lord" (Heb 12:14).